Contributors

Christine Flinn has many years' experience as a professional cake decorator, and has been ranked as one of the most skilled in royal icing in the UK. As a member of the British Sugarcraft Guild since 1984, she has won many gold certificates and trophies. Christine became an Accredited Demonstrator for the British Sugarcraft Guild in 1989, and since then she has earned her living creating designer cakes to order, teaching cake decoration and demonstrating sugarcraft techniques. Piping is her speciality, and she travels extensively throughout the UK, USA, Italy and Australia, running workshops and demonstrations.
  Visit Christine's website at www.christineflinn.co.uk

Having previously won Origin's Celebrity Crafter of the Year award, Stephanie Weightman now shares her expertise on television where she is a popular guest presenter and personality. She has worked with big-name craft products and developed many new products over the years and she regularly appears on air and online. She runs national creative workshops, appears at major shows and events and has written several books.
  Visit Stephanie's website at www.crafting.co.uk

In 2000, Sandra Monger left her job as a Registered Nurse to follow her life-long passion for baking and cake decoration. She studied an array of sugarcraft courses under the tutelage of sugarcraft guru Stephen Benison, and in 2002 established her own business. Sandra went on to become the City of Bath's premier wedding and celebration cake designer and the recommended supplier to some of the leading venues in the South West. Not content to keep her skills to herself, Sandra began teaching sugarcraft in 2007. Since 2008 she has designed and run a range of popular sugarcraft and cake decoration courses as well as running her successful business.
  Visit Sandra's website at www.sandramongercakes.co.uk

CAKE DECORATING
for Beginners

First published in 2019

Search Press Limited
Wellwood, North Farm Road,
Tunbridge Wells, Kent TN2 3DR

Reprinted 2020

Cake Decorating for Beginners uses material from the following books
published by Search Press:

Painting Flowers on Cakes by Stephanie Weightman, 2013
Stencilling on Cakes by Stephanie Weightman, 2013
Using Cutters on Cakes by Sandra Monger, 2014
Piping on Cakes by Christine Flinn, 2015

Text copyright © Stephanie Weightman, Sandra Monger and
Christine Flinn, 2019

Photographs by Paul Bricknell at Search Press Studios, except for
pages 6, 10, 16–17, 30, 42–53, 80–83, 124–127, 132–137, 146–149:
photographs by Roddy Paine Photographic Studios.

Photographs and design copyright © Search Press Ltd 2019

ISBN: 978-1-78221-754-1

Suppliers

If you have difficulty in obtaining any of the materials and equipment
mentioned in this book, please visit the Search Press website for details of
suppliers: www.searchpress.com

CAKE DECORATING
for Beginners

24 STUNNING STEP-BY-STEP CAKE DESIGNS
FOR ALL OCCASIONS

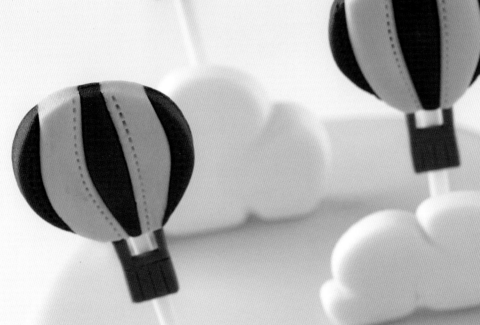

SEARCH PRESS

CONTENTS

Sunflower Cake 50

Toy Train 54

Indian Inlaid Cake 58

Flower Border 66

Modern Blackwork 72

Poppy Cake 80

Chocolate Heart 84

Hot-air Balloons 86

Rose Basket 90

Scrolls and Roses 98

Trellis Cake 106

Cameo Cake 108

MATERIALS AND TOOLS

CAKE AND CAKE TINS

When it comes to decorating cakes, fruit cake is the most traditional style that comes to mind. **Fruit cakes** are normally quite heavy and dense with a relatively low flour but high fruit content, and this cake stores well.

A basic **Victoria sandwich** recipe is buttery, spongy and light. It is perfect for large, small or cupcake-sized cakes and can be cut and shaped when cool. This delicate cake can be flavoured with vanilla extract or orange or lemon zest.

Chocolate cake can be light and fluffy or dense and moist and doesn't often last long enough to worry about storage, but it will normally keep well for four to five days.

Cake tins come in all shapes and sizes. Some are coated with a non-stick surface and some require you to line the tin or use paper cases; check your recipe for the most suitable method. If you are only going to use a special shaped tin once, consider hiring it from your local cake decorating shop.

A **turntable** is extremely useful, although not essential, when cake decorating. Choose one that has a tilting feature if possible.

Keep a variety of **cupcake cases** in your store cupboard, as they can be the finishing touch when it comes to coordinating the cake design with table decorations.

Cake boards are used to present celebration cakes on. The board is normally covered with icing and the edge with ribbon to complement your design.

A square Victoria sandwich, a fruit cake, chocolate cake and cupcakes.

CUTTING AND EMBELLISHING TOOLS

Cutters are most commonly used to cut a given shape, such as a circle, square, heart or star. Some cutters have a built-in sprung plunger that both embosses a pattern and removes the cut shape.

Wheel and parallel-wheel cutters are used for cutting round templates and to form lengths of decorative coverings of consistent width. These cutters reduce distortion and stretching of paste when it is being cut.

Other items can be used as cutters. These include **knives, pizza wheels, scissors, pinking shears** and **stationery punches**. Try experimenting with different items and see what works.

Embellishers are used to add pattern, texture and expression to cut-out shapes and cake surfaces. Specialist sugarcraft embellishers include **silicone veiners, moulds, stitching wheels** and **wheel embossers**. Household items can also be used to create new and individual effects – for example, scouring pads and brushes.

PIPING MATERIALS AND TOOLS

The best piping nozzles are seamless. These are not cheap, but if looked after, they will last a lifetime. Piping nozzles should always be washed by hand using a nozzle brush; never place them in a dishwasher. The tips are very delicate, so the nozzles should be stored in a box fitted with dividers so they will not rattle around. On no account should a pin or anything similar be inserted into the tip of the nozzle, as this will damage it and it will never pipe a true straight line again. Seamed nozzles can cause various problems including a piped line that curls or twists. Shown below, clockwise from top left are:

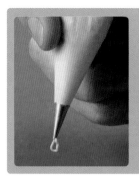

Tip

If the tip of a nozzle is damaged or partially blocked, when you are trying to pipe with it, the piped line will curl back on itself.

Piping bag holder Keeps the tip of the piping nozzle damp, as well as keeping the piping bags in order.

Parchment piping bags Four sizes are shown, to go with to the size of the piping nozzles.

Edible liquid food colours (droplets) These blend into any form of icing which is suitable for a piping bag.

Pipettes and shot glass Ideal for reconstituting pure powder food colour before adding to royal icing.

Pure powder food colour These are not petal dust. They are ideal when strong colours are required in royal icing.

Baking parchment (cut into triangles) Various sizes for creating piping bags.

Plastic side scraper Used as a surface on which to paddle small quantities of royal icing. Larger quantities of royal icing can be smoothed over a cake drum using a metal side scraper.

Disposable plastic piping bags The 30cm (12in) size is used with the piping nozzle adapter and the grass nozzle.

Piping nozzle adapter and **grass nozzle**

Knee-highs (**pop socks**) – used to sieve small quantities of royal icing when using fine or ultrafine piping nozzles (1, 0, or 00).

Nozzle brush Designed to clean a piping nozzle without damaging it.

Paper scissors Paper blunts scissors, so keep a pair of scissors just for that purpose.

Fine sable paintbrushes Natural bristle brushes which are soft but firm. They can be reshaped from a point to a flat tip and then back again.

Palette knives in 10cm (4in) and 20cm (8in).

Piping nozzles and subdivided **nozzle box** – it is vital to look after piping nozzles.

STENCILLING MATERIALS AND TOOLS

When using stencils, sometimes known as templates, to decorate your cakes, hygiene must be considered, so stencils should be made from food grade plastic or material and cleaned after every application. The ready-made stencils used in this book are available through all good stockists.

If you are cutting your own stencils (see page 31) they need to be made from **acetate** which is readily available from most craft shops. You will also need a **glass (or otherwise heatproof) mat** and a **stencil cutter** which can be bought from a general craft shop. Always plan your stencil design before attempting to cut out, find an image you would like to use and print it out so you can trace it using the stencil cutter, you need to make sure there are enough bridges in the stencil to stop the design falling apart.

You will need a **roller** to create a perfectly smooth surface on your cake prior to decorating and to emboss the stencils into the surface. **Rolling pins** come in lots of different sizes. Plastic ones are easy to keep clean and being straight, do not leave marks on the icing. White vegetable fat is used to prevent icing from sticking to your work surface when you roll it out: smooth a small amount on to the work surface before you start.

Spacers are lengths of plastic laid on the surface next to your icing. You then roll the roller over them to ensure an even thickness to your icing.

PAINTING MATERIALS AND TOOLS

Edible powder food colours can be mixed with edible confectionery glaze or varnish to create edible paint. These paints can be mixed using the techniques shown in this book, to create an infinite range of shades.

Palettes are perfect for keeping colours separate.

Nylon bristle brushes are the most hygienic for painting on cakes. You will need a variety of sizes for the projects in this book: round brushes in sizes 1, 2, 5, 6 and 9 and flat brushes in 15mm (⅝in), 10mm (⅜in), 6mm (¼in) and 2mm (⅛in). You should clean the brushes between each application to stop the colours from becoming muddy.

Food grade alcohol or **isopropyl** is used to clean brushes and remove edible varnish.

Edible lustre spray can be sprayed on to sugarpaste (fondant), sugar sheets, chocolate, buttercream and marzipan to create stunning lustre effects.

There are two kinds of **glitter** available to cake decorators: both are non-toxic, but one needs to be removed from your cake before eating, while the other is fully edible. Please check your glitter pot before applying to your cake.

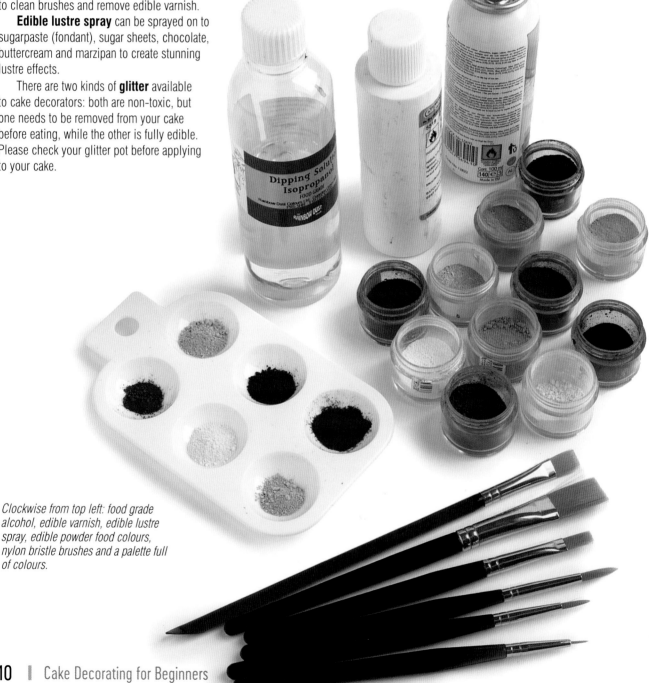

Clockwise from top left: food grade alcohol, edible varnish, edible lustre spray, edible powder food colours, nylon bristle brushes and a palette full of colours.

OTHER MATERIALS AND TOOLS

In addition to the main materials listed on the previous pages, you will need a few other items:

Craft punches are a good alternative to decorating with ribbon when used in conjunction with sugar sheets.

Greaseproof paper protects surfaces and is used to line cake tins.

Rulers are used both for measuring and making straight line impressions.

Palette knives in various sizes are used to lift rolled icing on to cupcakes and cakes and also to smooth royal icing or buttercream.

A **pastry brush** can be used to brush fruit preserves on to cakes.

Various sizes of **scissors** are useful to cut sugarpaste (fondant) sheets and baking parchment. Scissors with a non-stick coating are ideal.

Edible glue is used to stick two icing surfaces together

Kitchen paper is used to dry brushes and clean up.

Cake boards are used to present celebration cakes. The board is normally covered with icing and edged with ribbon to complement your design.

A **worktop or food board** with non-slip backing is essential.

Masking tape is useful to secure stencils in place.

A **sharp kitchen knife** can be used to cut through icing without leaving rough edges.

Various widths, colours and designs of **ribbon** are used for decorating cake bases and boards.

Smeared in a thin layer, **white vegetable fat** helps prevent icing sticking to your surfaces.

If you have a selection of coloured icing, a variety of **small bowls** to keep the colours separate is useful.

Sticky tape or low-tack sticky tape is used to attach ribbons to the surface of cake boards for a perfect finish.

A **smoother** is a flat-faced tool you can use over the surface of your cake to create a perfect finish.

A **craft knife** is always useful in cake decoration for fine details.

String is used to help measure around large cakes when stencilling the sides.

Use **glass-headed pins** to temporarily secure ribbons or stencils in place on cakes. You can cover any holes they leave with a small amount of icing and a little water.

A **powder dredger** is used to sprinkle icing sugar on to surfaces prior to rolling out, and also to dust cocoa on to stencils.

A **shaping mat** is a bumpy foam mat used to help develop the shapes of small sugarpaste (fondant) pieces.

CAKE COVERINGS AND EDIBLES

The main covering for both cakes and boards in this book is **sugarpaste (fondant) icing**. It can be bought ready to roll (although usually requires a little kneading) and in a range of colours. It can also be coloured with edible paste colour. Sugarpaste (fondant) can also be used as a modelling material if it is strengthened (see opposite) and can be textured and embellished.

Marzipan is a paste made of almonds and sugar. It can be used as a cake covering for a traditional fruit cake, where it forms a layer under the outer sugarpaste (fondant) covering. It can also be used as a modelling material and as a filling for sweets and cakes.

Modelling paste is made by adding a strengthening agent to sugarpaste (fondant) to make it pliable and elastic. It dries a little stronger than sugarpaste (fondant) and is used where decorative items are required to hold their shape. It can be made at home or is available from sugarcraft suppliers.

Gum paste (also known as **flower paste**) can be used for moulding and forming delicate shapes such as petals. It can be made at home or is available from sugarcraft suppliers.

Royal icing can be used to fix decorative items in position. It is also a cake covering in its own right and can be used for piping borders, patterns and decorations.

Jam (also known as **jelly**) is used as a cake filling in traditional sponge cakes. Apricot jam (jelly) is often used as a sticking agent when covering a fruit cake with marzipan, though any flavour, or even marmalade, can be used instead. Always boil the jam (jelly) before using – this kills any mould spores that may be present.

OTHER EDIBLES

Other edibles can be used for colouring, enhancing, patterning and embellishing. These can include paste and powder colours, confectionery glazes, lustres and glitters, sugar- and rice-paper transfer sheets, and edible sprinkles, gems and dragees.

Strengthening agents such as CMC powder (also known as tylose) and gum tragacanth powder are used to give decorative pastes pliability, stretch and strength, making them suitable for flower making and modelling. CMC is a synthetic cellulose gum whilst gum tragacanth powder is a natural substance derived from the gum of several species of shrub. Both powders take six to twelve hourvs to work when added to a paste, so they are usually best left to rest overnight. They will need to be stored in an airtight plastic bag to prevent drying.

Dipping solution is used in sugarcraft for creating glazes, and combining lustre and powder colours into a solution. It is also used for cleaning brushes after a glaze has been used. It is sometimes known as rejuvenator spirit or glaze cleaner. It contains isopropyl alcohol.

COLOURING PASTE

Gum paste (flower paste) and modelling paste can be coloured using edible paste colour.

1. Knead the paste to warm and soften it, then pick up a tiny amount of colour on a cocktail stick and transfer it to the paste.

2. Knead the colour into the paste until you obtain an even colour. Remember: you can always add more colour, but you can't take it away, so add it in small increments.

3. To obtain a marbled effect, simply knead the paste until you achieve the required effect.

TECHNIQUES

COVERING YOUR CAKE

A perfectly covered cake is an ideal surface to decorate. Covering your chosen cake with sugarpaste (fondant) will help to give you a professional-looking smooth base.

COVERING A CAKE WITH SUGARPASTE (FONDANT)

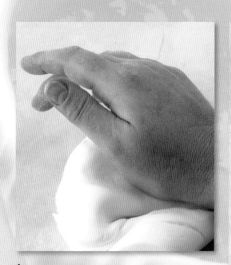

1. Knead the sugarpaste (fondant) using the heel of your hand until it becomes smooth and workable.

2. Cover the surface with white vegetable fat, then put down your spacers (see inset) and roll out the sugarpaste (fondant). The spacers help to ensure you get a uniform thickness to the icing.

3. Cover the cake so that there is a small skirt of icing around every edge as shown.

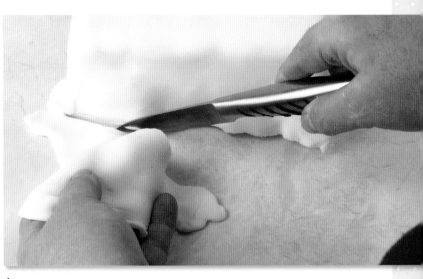

4. Pull in the skirt and trim it away using a sharp knife.

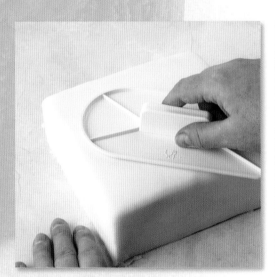

5. Using a smoother, smooth the icing over the whole cake. Trim away any excess from the bottom, if necessary, using a sharp kitchen knife.

The covered cake in place on a cake board.

COVERING A CAKE WITH MARZIPAN AND ROYAL ICING

Royal icing needs a really smooth surface, and marzipan is not only tasty; it is also ideal on top of a fruit cake to smooth out any little bumps before the royal icing is applied. Alternatively, you can use pouring fondant to achieve the same effect.

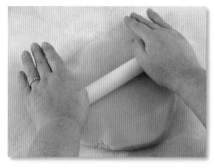

1. Sprinkle icing sugar on your work surface. Knead the marzipan and roll it out to a size large enough to cover the whole cake with some to spare.

2. Brush apricot jam (jelly) over the fruit cake using a pastry brush.

3. Lift the marzipan on a large rolling pin, supporting it with your hand, and place it over the cake.

4. The cake now has a marzipan 'skirt'. Trim this with a knife.

5. Press the marzipan into the cake using your hands and trim it again.

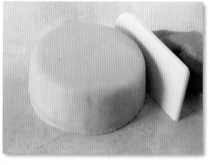

6. Smooth the surface of the marzipan with a smoother.

7. Place greaseproof paper on a turntable and place the cake on top. Spoon the royal icing on top of the cake.

8. Turn the cake and allow the royal icing to run down the sides, helping it into place with a wooden spoon.

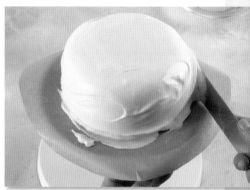

10. Wet the palette knife again and continue turning the cake and smoothing the icing. Scrape off the icing that sticks to the palette knife each time you wet it in the hot water.

9. Place a bowl of hot water beside you and wet the palette knife in it. Smooth the royal icing with it, turning the cake as you go.

11. Continue in the same way, smoothing and resmoothing the icing. Towards the end of the process you are aiming to create sharp edges and a neat finish at the bottom.

Tip

For a professional finish, try applying three coats of royal icing to the top and the sides of the cake separately.

The iced cake.

COATING A SQUARE CAKE DRUM WITH ROYAL ICING

A coated cake drum always creates a professional look to
a finished celebration cake.

1. Apply a small amount of royal icing (normal consistency) to the
cake drum, and paddle it with the palette knife, adding more until it
is completely covered.

2. Hold the edge of a metal side scraper level with the cake drum
and, in one smooth action, pull it along the cake drum. Turn the
cake on the turntable and repeat the action on the remaining sides.
For a chamfered cake drum, use a flexi-scraper.

3. Use small, downward cutting actions with the palette knife to
remove the surplus royal icing at the edges of the cake drum. Wipe
the blade with a clean, damp cloth on each action. Clean the edge
of the cake drum with the clean, damp cloth. Leave the royal icing
to dry for no less than four hours before continuing.

4. Place a small amount of
royal icing in a glass jug
or bowl. Add a little water
to create a thick run sugar
consistency. Cover the bowl
with a damp cloth and leave to
stand for no less than fifteen
minutes before continuing.
Cut through the air pockets
(bubbles) on the surface of the
royal icing with a knife.

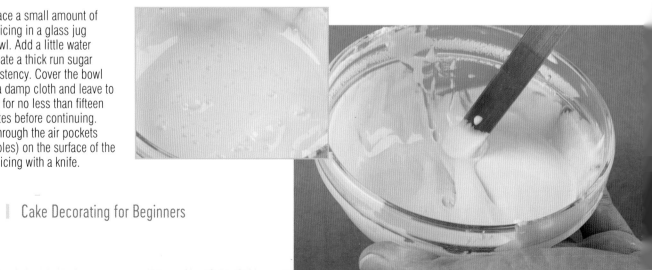

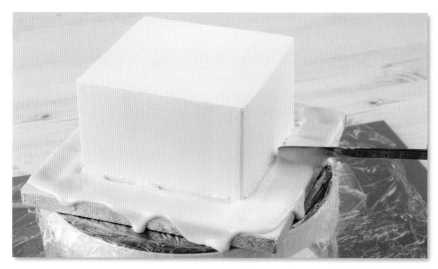

5. Cover the turntable with a piece of plastic food wrap. Apply the run sugar to the coated cake drum and continue applying more it until it is completely covered.

6. Hold the edge of a metal side scraper level with the cake drum and in one smooth action, pull the scraper along the cake drum. Turn the cake on the turntable and repeat the action on the remaining sides. For a chamfered cake drum, use a flexi-scraper.

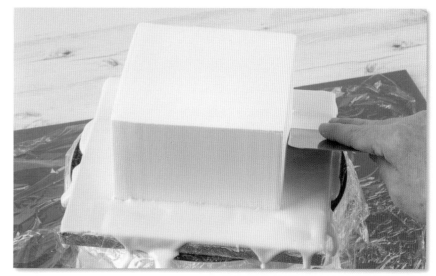

7. Clean up the side edge of the cake drum using a palette knife and a clean, damp cloth. Leave the run-sugar coated cake drum to dry completely (twenty-four hours) before commencing the piped decoration.

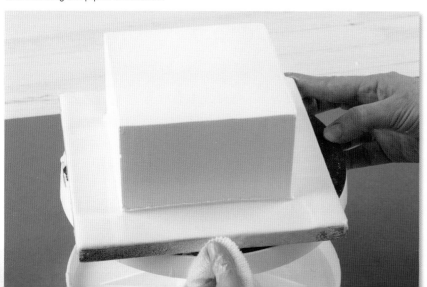

Covering a round cake drum

This is the same as a square cake drum, but the levelling with the metal side scraper needs to be done in one smooth action – so hold the turntable edge and turn it the same way as you would for smoothing the coating at the sides of a round cake.

COVERING A CAKE DRUM WITH SUGARPASTE (FONDANT) – THE BANDAGE METHOD

An iced cake drum creates a more professional look to the finished celebration cake.
Dampen the cake drum with water before beginning.

1. Roll a piece of sugarpaste (fondant) into a long sausage.Lightly dust the work surface with icing sugar (powdered sugar) and roll out the sausage until it is approximately 3mm (1/8in) thick. Cut one of the long edges straight.

2. Roll up the strip of sugarpaste (fondant) like a bandage.

3. Carefully unwind the bandage around the cake with the cut edge towards the cake. Ease it into position and don't unroll too much at once.

4. Overlap the sugarpaste (fondant) where it meets and cut through both layers. Remove the surplus and rub with your thumbs to smooth the join.

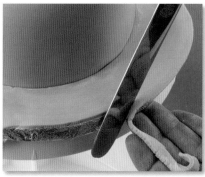

5. Trim the sugarpaste (fondant) which is overhanging the cake drum.

6. Rub the cut edge around the edge of the cake drum with the side of your hand to smooth it.

Option

At this stage, you can emboss the edge of the sugarpaste (fondant) on the cake drum with a design of your choice.

COVERING MINI CAKES AND CUPCAKES

To cover mini cakes, follow the same method as for large cakes but use a slightly thinner covering.

Cupcakes can be covered with a variety of toppings such as ganache, buttercream, jam (jelly) and sugarpaste (fondant), and finished with decorative items formed from a range of materials. Why not add a delicious surprise in the form of a hidden filling?

1. If you wish to add a filling, scoop out a little hole and add some jam (jelly) or buttercream (or both) before adding a covering to the cake.

2. Spread the filling thinly over the top of the cake too. This will provide something for the cake covering to stick on to.

3. Knead a little sugarpaste (fondant) to soften, then sprinkle some icing sugar on your worksurface and roll the sugarpaste (fondant) out thinly.

4. Choose a circle cutter that is slightly smaller than the top of your cake and cut out a circle.

5. .Place the sugarpaste (fondant) circle on top of the cake.

6. Smooth the surface of the sugarpaste (fondant) covering gently with your fingers.

Tip

Any unused pieces of sugarpaste (fondant) can be rolled up and stored in a plastic bag for future use, providing it is clean and does not have cake crumbs or buttercream attached to it. It does not need to be stored in a refrigerator.

DECORATING YOUR CAKE

MOULDING AND SHAPING TECHNIQUES

Decorative elements made using cutters can be shaped and moulded into different forms. This can be done by hand or using a variety of items to cup, bend, fold and adapt them. Here are some simple shapes to get you started.

MAKING CLOUDS

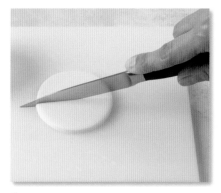

1. Roll out the modelling paste and cut out a circle using a metal circle cutter. Cut the circle in half cleanly with a sharp knife.

2. Use the corner of a square cutter to 'nip' out the points of the cloud.

3. Shape and smooth the points with your finger to make a cloud shape.

WRAPPING STRIPS ROUND A SHAPE

Cut the strips using a parallel wheel cutter (ribbon cutter). Curve the first strip round the shape, then continue outwards with the other strips. Work quickly to avoid the paste drying out. Trim the ends of the strips using a sharp knife.

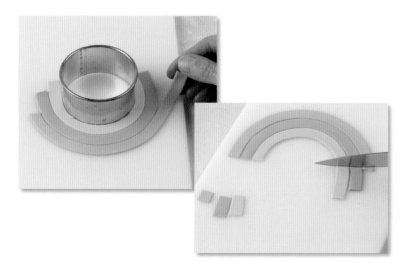

MAKING THREE-DIMENSIONAL SHAPES

Form a lump of paste into a ball of the required depth, and cut out the shape using a metal cutter. Push the paste out of the cutter using the end of a non-stick rolling pin.

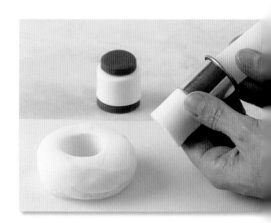

SHAPING LARGE FLOWERS

1. To make simple, unfrilled, cupped flower shapes, rub a little vegetable shortening over the surface of a former (this can be any curved shape). Cut out a flower and lay it over the former. Gently press it down onto the surface and leave to dry overnight.

2. To add more movement to simple flower shapes, place the flower on a foam mat and rub the centre of each petal in a firm, circular motion using a ball tool. Rub the edges of the petals in the same way to give them a thin, wavy edge.

3. Flower shapes can also be layered. Separate the petals using small, torn pieces of paper tissue and allow to dry. This will give the flower depth.

SHAPING SMALL FLOWERS

Use a plunger cutter to cut out the flower shapes and press them out onto a foam mat. Press down firmly into the foam mat as you do so. This will force the flower petals to curve upwards.

CUTTING TECHNIQUES

To use cutters effectively, you need to know how to handle them correctly and how to achieve consistent results, such as rolling pastes to an even thickness. Developing your cutter skills will enable you to use them in imaginative ways to create new shapes and forms, or as embellishers to give expression, pattern and texture to a decorative surface.

ROLLING OUT THE PASTE

Grease your rolling board with a tiny amount of vegetable shortening and roll out your paste between two metal rulers to achieve a very thin layer. Use a non-stick rolling pin.

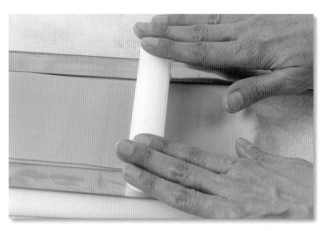

USING A KNIFE

Use a sharp kitchen knife, and cut the paste using a see-saw motion. Avoid dragging the knife through the paste. The length of knife you choose should be one that allows you to make a single cut in one movement. A pizza wheel can also be used for cutting shapes – it's particularly useful for cutting round circles.

USING A WHEEL CUTTER

Run the wheel cutter firmly along a hard edge, for example a metal ruler. Make the cut in a single movement; avoid going over the same edge twice.

USING A PIPING NOZZLE

A piping nozzle is useful for cutting out tiny shapes. It can also be used as an embellisher. Simply press the nozzle into the paste and push out the shape with a cocktail stick.

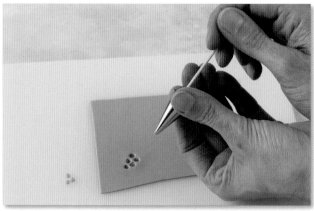

USING A PLUNGER CUTTER

Plunger cutters are quick and easy to use. They cut the shape and release it. Some even emboss a pattern.

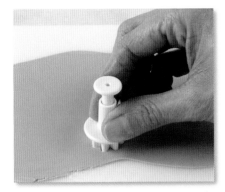

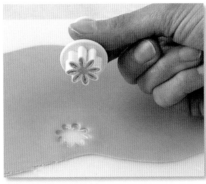

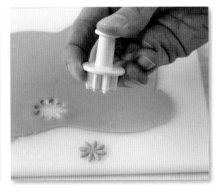

1. Sprinkle the board lightly with cornstarch (cornflour) then press the cutter firmly onto the paste. Press down on the cutter, not the plunger.

2. Lift the cutter cleanly away from the paste. The shape will be removed with it.

3. Press down on the plunger and the cut shape will drop out.

USING A METAL CUTTER

Metal cutters are generally sharper than plungers, but the shapes are not quite as easy to remove. Roll out your paste as before, position the metal cutter (sharp edge down) and press down on it firmly. Lift the cutter away cleanly and press out the shape carefully with your fingers or a paintbrush.

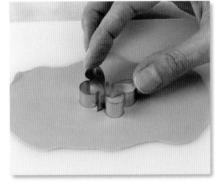

Tip

Always clean your cutter between uses using your fingers or a dry cloth to avoid mixing different colours.

USING A PARALLEL WHEEL CUTTER

Also known as a ribbon cutter, this is available with a variety of different edges, and is used to cut even strips of paste. Hold the wheel cutter by the handles on either side and roll it firmly along the paste in a straight line. Carefully lift away the paste on either side of the strip.

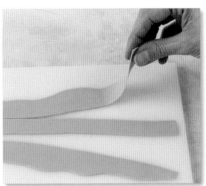

EMBELLISHING TECHNIQUES

Embellishing a decorative surface is an art in itself. From forming geometric patterns to creating naturalistic textures, embellishing goes hand-in-hand with using cutters.

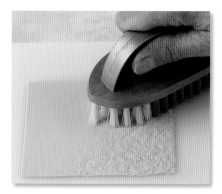

SCRUBBING BRUSH

Press down firmly onto the paste (don't rub) to create the effect of grass, mud and ground. The same effect can be achieved with a scouring pad.

EMBOSSING MAT

This is reversible and can be used to create either a raised or a recessed pattern. Lay the mat on the paste, roll over it firmly and carefully lift it off.

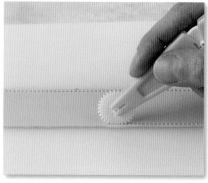

STITCHING WHEEL

Simply run the wheel carefully round the edge or over the surface of the paste to create a line that resembles stitching. Various designs are available.

SILICONE VEINER

Silicone veiners are soft and flexible tools used to create decorative impressions and reliefs on the surfaces of leaves and flowers. They are available in many varieties.

VARNISHING

Confectionery glaze can be painted onto the paste with a paintbrush. Make sure the paintbrush is cleaned thoroughly in dipping solution after use.

TRANSFER SHEET

Transfer sheets are printed, edible rice paper. Simply remove the backing, lightly moisten the paste, and apply the transfer. Smooth it into place with your fingers.

PIPING TECHNIQUES

MAKING A PIPING BAG

Paper piping bags are essential for good piping. No fewer than four sizes are required. Baking parchment is a better choice than greaseproof paper.

- Cut a rectangular piece of baking parchment:

Size 1 (extra small): 25.4 x 15.2cm (10 x 6in)

Size 2 (small): 30.5 x 20.3cm (12 x 8in)

Size 3 (medium): 30.5 x 33cm (12 x 13in)

Size 4 (large) 45.7cm (18 x 15in)

- Fold the piece of paper in half diagonally to make a triangle (with one flat end – not pointed).

- Cut the paper along the fold line.

PIPING NOZZLE INFORMATION

Different manufacturers label the piping nozzles in different ways when it comes to the size of the opening and the type (plain or serrated). The sizes and diameters of the nozzles used for the most intricate piping in this book are approximately as follows:

No. 0: 0.25mm ($\frac{1}{128}$in)

No. 1: 0.5mm ($\frac{1}{64}$in)

No. 1.5: 0.75mm ($\frac{1}{32}$in)

No. 2: 1mm ($\frac{1}{16}$in)

No. 3: 2.25mm ($\frac{3}{32}$in)

No. 4: 2.5mm ($\frac{5}{64}$in)

Golden rules

- Always paddle the royal icing with a backwards and forwards movement of the palette knife, to displace air bubbles.
- Always use the right size of piping bag for the size of the piping nozzle or tip.
- The smaller the piping nozzle, the softer the royal icing needs to be.
- Never more than half-fill a piping bag. If you overfill the piping bag, your hand will ache and the piping bag might burst.
- Don't use a piping bag for any longer than thirty minutes, as the heat from your hand will cause the royal icing to firm up, making it harder to pipe. The consistency will also become short or brittle.

MAKING PIPED ROSES

When piping roses, it is best to work on several at the same time, as this allows a small amount of drying time between layers. You will need a no. 57 petal nozzle, but if you are left-handed, make sure it is a left-handed nozzle, and reverse the direction for turning the cocktail stick (so clockwise becomes anticlockwise).

You will need

Piping bag (size 3)
No. 57 nozzle
Cocktail sticks
Wax paper

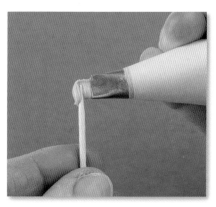

1. Hold the piping bag in one hand and a cocktail stick in the other. The narrow end of the nozzle needs to be at a fraction higher than the tip of the cocktail stick. Touch the cocktail stick to start and apply pressure to the piping bag, turning the cocktail stick at the same time. Pipe a tight spiral (it should not have an open centre).

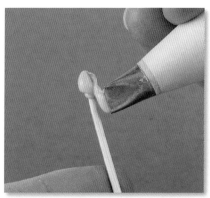

2. To finish the spiral, bring the nozzle down in a sweeping action and finish on the cocktail stick.

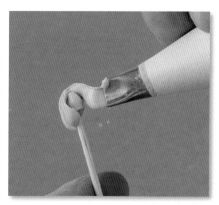

3. Pipe the next petal (one of three). Touch the cocktail stick to start each petal. In a clockwise direction, pipe the petal in a horse-shoe shape while slowly turning the cocktail stick. Finish the petal by touching the cocktail stick.

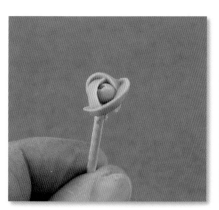

4. Repeat step 3 with the remaining two petals. Each petal should overlap the previous one and the last petal should overlap the first.

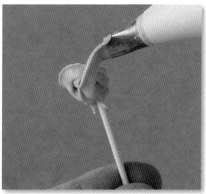

5. Pipe the next five petals in the same way as the previous three, but this time in an anticlockwise direction.

The completed rose.

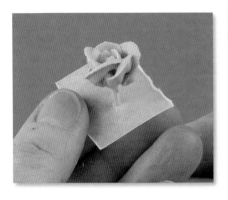

6. Feed the cocktail stick through a small square of wax paper and remove the rose.

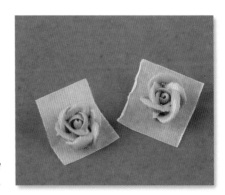

7. Leave the roses to dry completely.

MAKING A LEAF NOZZLE AND PIPING THE CALYX

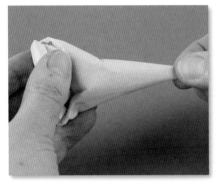

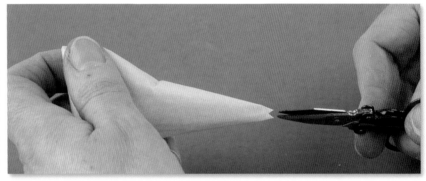

8. Create a piping bag (size 2) but give it an extra half twist to make it narrower. Half fill it with royal icing which has been coloured green. Fold the top of the piping bag over as normal to make a neat, tidy parcel. Squash the tip of the piping bag flat with your index finger and thumb.

9. Using fine scissors, cut a small inverted 'V' from the tip of the piping bag.

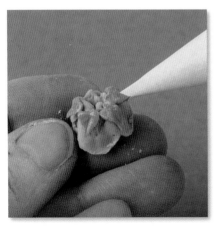

10. Pipe five small leaf shapes on the base of the piped rose to create the calyx. Leave to dry.

The finished piped rose with its calyx.

USING SUGAR SHEETS

Sugar sheets are so useful; they can be painted in advance, stored in a sealed bag and cut out before or after storage.

MAKING AND DECORATING A PLAQUE

1. Peel the backing off a sugar sheet. Paint a rose on a sugar sheet as shown on page 46. Cover a cupcake in buttercream. Use a cutter to cut out a plaque around the rose.

2. Place the rose plaque on the cupcake.

3. Apply more buttercream in the middle of the first rose.

4. Paint two leaves on sugar sheets, one with one scalloped side (see page 44) and one scalloped (see page 43). Cut out the leaves using scissors.

5. Stick the leaves in the buttercream, then add another rose on top.

The finished cupcake.

MAKING A BORDER

Decorative borders can be punched from sugar sheets and attached using edible glue.

1. Peel the backing off the sugar sheet and place a strip in a border punch. Punch out the shape, moving along the sheet as you go.

2. Place the border on greaseproof paper and spray it with lustre spray.

STENCILLING TECHNIQUES

There is a variety of ways to use stencils in cake decoration, from creating simple embossing to sumptuous blended colour effects. All sorts of icing, ganache, chocolate and even buttercream can be used with stencils to great effect, and with the right equipment you can cut your own stencils to create unique and individual designs.

CUTTING YOUR OWN STENCILS

1. With a glass mat to protect your work surface, place a sheet of acetate over your template.

2. Use low-tack tape to secure the acetate to the template while your hot stencil cutting tool is warming up. Next, use the tool like a pen to draw round the template.

3. Continue drawing round every detail of the template until you have finished. Remove the tape and then carefully lift the cut-out template away.

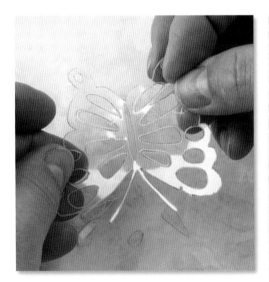

4. You may need to remove internal parts of the template. If so, simply pull them gently until they come away. As long as you have cut round them, they should come out easily.

A completed stencil.

EMBOSSING

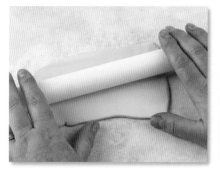

1. Lay a thin layer of white vegetable fat over the work surface, then knead a small amount of sugarpaste (fondant) and roll it out to a thickness of no less than 5mm (¼in) using a small rolling pin.

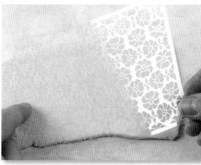

2. Carefully lay the embossing stencil flat on top of the icing.

3. Roll the small rolling pin firmly over the stencil and sugarpaste (fondant).

4. Peel away the stencil carefully.

A cupcake covered with embossed sugarpaste (fondant).

DUSTING

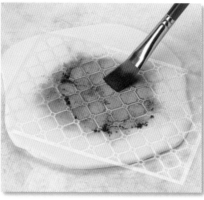

1. Follow steps one and two for embossing (see opposite), and leave the stencil in place.

2. Lightly brush a contrasting colour of edible dusting powder over the whole piece using a soft flat brush. Aim to cover a piece slightly larger than the size of your cutter.

3. Continue brushing the powder into the surface until it has all been worked in; this ensures the piece will remain clean when you lift away the stencil.

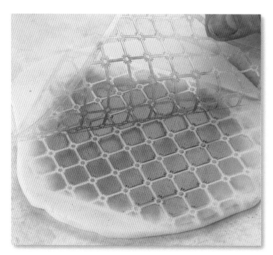

4. Carefully peel away the stencil.

A cupcake covered with embossed and dusted sugarpaste (fondant).

BLENDING COLOURS

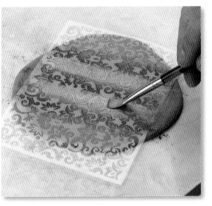

1. Follow steps one and two for embossing (see page 32), and leave the stencil in place. Brush on your first colour of edible dusting powder in bold stripes.

2. Change to a clean brush and brush on a complementary colour of edible dusting powder between the stripes.

3. Still using the brush with the second colour, blend the boundaries of the stripes together until all the powder has been worked in.

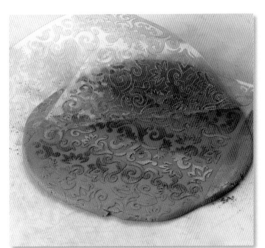

4. Peel the stencil away carefully.

A cupcake covered with embossed sugarpaste (fondant) coloured with blended gold and purple.

PICKING OUT ELEMENTS OF A DESIGN

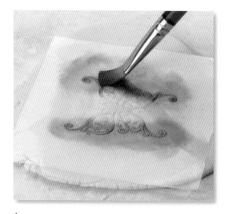

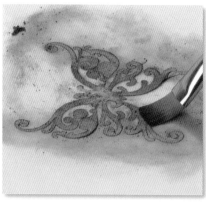

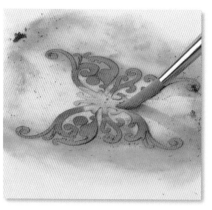

1. Follow steps one and two for embossing (see page 32), and leave the stencil in place. Using a small flat brush and your first colour of edible dusting powder, pick out some of the details of the design, working from the outside of the stencil inwards. In this instance, use metallic pink.

2. Using a clean brush and a second colour (mulberry here), work closer towards the centre of the design, blending the powder into the previous colour.

3. Blend in a third colour (metallic purple here) to the central part of the design. Use a size 5 clean round brush to pick out any small details.

4. Gently brush any excess powder away from the design, being careful not to blur the image, then peel away the stencil.

A cupcake decorated with sugarpaste (fondant) and a decorative butterfly.

CUTTING OUT A STENCILLED DESIGN

1. Follow steps 1–4 for blending (see page 34) using electric blue and metallic light silver edible dusting powders.

2. Hold a sharp craft knife with a clean disposable blade perpendicular to the surface. Begin to trim carefully around the design, working up to the edges.

3. Cut away large sections of excess sugarpaste (fondant) to make it easier to cut closely to the design.

4. Use a palette knife to carefully lift the whole design away from the surface, ready to use.

A square cake covered with sugarpaste (fondant), with a sugarpaste design in place.

STENCILLING ON BUTTERCREAM

1. Mix your buttercream and apply a layer to the top of the cupcake. Smooth it using a warm palette knife, then place it in the refrigerator until it hardens and forms a crust.

2. Gently place the stencil on top of the cupcake.

3. Using a powder dredger filled with cocoa powder, dust the cake thoroughly.

4. Cover the whole cake (see inset) then carefully lift away the stencil.

A cupcake covered with chocolate-decorated buttercream.

PLACING A DESIGN ON THE SIDE OF A CAKE

1. Place the stencil on the side of the cake and use pins to hold it in place temporarily.

2. Mix melted chocolate and double cream to make chocolate ganache, and use a palette knife to apply a fairly large amount to the centre of the stencil.

3. Remove the pins and use the palette knife to spread the ganache thinly over the whole area.

4. Carefully peel away the stencil to reveal the pattern.

A square cake covered with sugarpaste (fondant), with a stencilled design in chocolate ganache on one side.

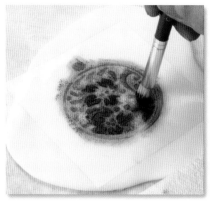

1. Follow steps one and two for embossing (see page 32), and leave the stencil in place. Pick up green colouring gel on a medium (size 2) stencilling brush and stipple it on to a piece of kitchen paper to remove the excess gel.

2. Very softly stipple over the whole stencil except for the flower petals, as shown.

3. Load a clean size 2 stencilling brush with red colouring gel. Stipple it on to a piece of kitchen paper as before to remove excess gel, then very lightly stipple the flower petals.

4. Carefully lift away the stencil.

A cupcake covered with sugarpaste (fondant), decorated with wet colouring gel.

1. Using scissors, carefully trim away any border on your stencil.

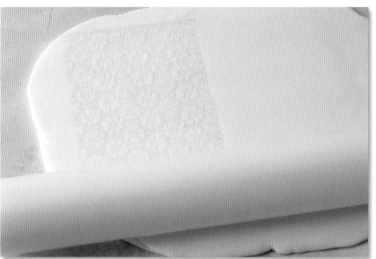

2. Knead white sugarpaste (fondant) using the heel of your hand until it becomes smooth and workable, then cover the surface with white vegetable fat, put down your spacers and roll out the sugarpaste (fondant). Place your stencil on top and roll firmly over it with a large rolling pin.

3. Carefully remove the stencil, then replace it, matching the existing embossed detail to the detail on the stencil to help you position it perfectly in place.

4. Use a small rolling pin with a chamfered edge to roll firmly over the stencil, being careful not to roll over the previously embossed detail.

5. Carefully remove the stencil and repeat the process to the end of the icing.

6. Using a spacer as a straight edge, cut away the excess icing with a sharp kitchen knife.

The completed sheet of embossed sugarpaste (fondant).

PAINTING TECHNIQUES

A few simple strokes create designs with the wow factor if you use these simple techniques. The most important part of the whole painting process is brush loading. If the brush runs out of paint, make sure it is reloaded perfectly before continuing. If the colours look muddy, you may have used too much liquid, so dry your brush and reload it with colour.

Painting tip

You should always paint at eye level, so place books under your turntable when you paint near the bottom of a cake, and take them out as you paint higher up.

PREPARING TO PAINT

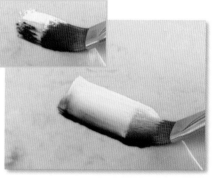

1. Dip a 10mm (⅜in) flat brush in edible varnish.

2. Dip one corner of the brush in white edible powder food colour, then dip the other corner in green colour so that the brush is double-loaded.

3. Brush on to a sheet of acetate until the grains of powder are crushed into the varnish, making a smooth, workable edible paint in two shades.

MAKING A FLAT LEAF BRUSH STROKE

1. On your sugar surface, paint a brush stroke, going slightly upwards to start with, then curve down.

2. Flick upwards with the straight edge of the brush to finish the leaf shape.

The finished flat leaf.

MAKING A SCALLOPED LEAF SHAPE

1. Double-load the brush with green and white as before, crush the grains, then wiggle the brush on the sugar surface to create the scalloped shape.

2. Paint a smooth shape and curve up to finish the first half of the leaf.

3. Complete the lower half of the leaf in the same way, but as a mirror image.

The finished leaf.

4. Slide the edge of the brush into the leaf to paint a curved stem.

MAKING A SMOOTH LEAF SHAPE

1. Paint a stroke as for the flat leaf shape.

2. Repeat as a mirror image to complete the lower half of the leaf.

3. Add a stem as for the scalloped leaf.

The finished leaf.

PAINTING A LEAF WITH ONE SCALLOPED SIDE

1. Paint the top of the leaf as for the scalloped leaf.

2. Paint the bottom half as for a smooth leaf, then add the stem.

The finished leaf.

PAINTING A POPPY LEAF

1. Wiggle the brush as for painting a scalloped leaf.

2. Continue the wiggle through several curves, then slide the brush out to a point.

3. Pick up more paint and repeat to paint the other side of the leaf.

4. Slide the brush out to a point.

5. Use the straight edge of the brush to paint a stem.

The finished leaf.

BRUSHING TOGETHER FLAT PETALS TO MAKE A FLOWER

1. Double-load the brush with red and white and paint a flat leaf shape (or in this case, a petal).

2. Paint another petal with the tip finishing at the same point, and continue round in a circle.

The finished flower.

PAINTING A SUNFLOWER

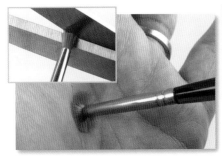

1. Take a cheap round nylon brush and cut across the bristles to customize it for stippling. Crush the bristles to splay them.

2. Pick up black and brown powder food colours and crush them on to the acetate. Paint the centre of the sunflower with the flat, cut part of the brush.

3. Change to the flat brush and double-load it with yellow and white. Stroke on petals, pulling out the dark colour of the centre.

4. Go once round the flower, then reload the brush with yellow and white and go over the petals again to brighten them.

5. Stipple over the edges of the centre to soften them in.

The finished sunflower.

PAINTING DOTS AND BERRIES

1. Pick up some varnish on the end of a brush handle and put it on the palette, then mix in red powder food colour.

2. Dot the berries on to the sugar surface using the end of the brush handle.

3. Mix white powder with the varnish in the same way and use a no. 1 round brush to dot on the highlights.

The finished berries.

PAINTING A ROSE

1. Double-load the brush with red and white, then paint a petal with a wiggling motion as for a scalloped leaf.

2. Continue round in a circle, adding petals to complete the first layer.

3. Inside the first layer, paint a smooth petal like a flat leaf.

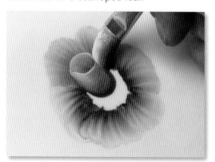

4. Paint the second smooth petal below the first to create the centre of the rose.

5. Paint the third smooth petal below this one.

6. Paint a smooth petal at the side of the centre.

7. Add another smooth petal the other side of the centre.

8. Paint a final smooth petal below the centre as shown.

The finished rose.

PAINTING A ROSEBUD

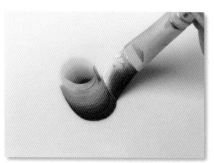

1. Repeat steps 3, 4 and 5 of the rose to create the bud.

2. Leave some colour on the brush and pick up green and white. Paint the first curve of the leaf as shown.

3. Paint a second leaf on the other side, then a third one in front.

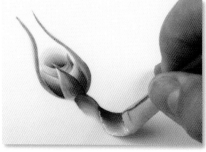

4. Paint the top of the stem with a curving stroke below the petal.

The finished rosebud.

PAINTING STEMS AND TENDRILS

1. Use the no. 1 brush double-loaded with green and white. Start with a fairly thick stroke and pull it out, tapering to a point.

2. Continue painting stems from the same point, then change to the no. 10 flat brush and begin to add flat leaves.

3. Use the no. 1 brush with green and paint a curling shape, tapering and allowing the colour to fade towards the end. Add several tendrils to the stems and leaves.

The stems with flat leaves.

The finished stems and leaves with tendrils.

PAINTING BOWS

1. Use the no. 10 flat brush with red and white and paint two loops as shown.

2. Paint two trailing ribbons from the centre of the bow.

3. Paint a stroke for the centre over the point where the loops meet.

The finished bow.

OUTLINING IN CHOCOLATE

Chocolate outlines are excellent for covering imperfections, so they might be popular when you first start painting on cakes. Try using chocolate in different colours.

OUTLINING A SUNFLOWER

1. Paint the sunflower on to a sugar sheet as shown on page 45. Make a small piping bag with greaseproof paper and fill it with melted chocolate. Pipe an outline around the sunflower.

2. Add a highlight in the centre.

OUTLINING A ROSEBUD

1. Paint a rosebud on sugarpaste (fondant) as shown on page 47. Pipe a leaf outline attached to the stem.

2. Fill in the leaf outline with piped chocolate.

The finished rosebud with a chocolate leaf.

SUNFLOWER CAKE

When a large celebration cake is called for, why not make a grand statement with this giant sunflower design? The size of the flower head can be adjusted to fit any size of cake from cupcake to extra large rounds. Trim the base of the cake and board with a wide yellow ribbon and add a brown one on top.

You will need

You will need
35.5cm (14in) cake covered in sugarpaste (fondant)
35.5cm (14in) cake board
Edible powder food colours in chocolate brown, white, soft yellow, bright yellow, burgundy
Edible varnish
Food grade alcohol
Brushes: 15mm (⅝in) flat, size 9 round
Wide yellow and narrow brown ribbons

1. Use the 15mm (⅝in) flat brush to paint a large circle for the centre of the sunflower in chocolate brown in the middle of the cake. Use large, sweeping strokes.

2. Double-load the brush with soft yellow and white and paint petals around the centre, without touching the brown.

3. Double-load with bright yellow and white and paint more petals in between the first ones.

4. Make sure you paint with random strokes, rather than going round in a circle from beginning to end, or you will end up with a 'windmill effect'.

5. Double-load with yellow and white and a little burgundy so that some petals have a darker edge.

Opposite

The finished sunflower cake. This is perfect for a summer occasion or for someone who loves their garden. The iced board is edged with a yellow and a brown ribbon.

6. Paint edible varnish over the sunflower centre.

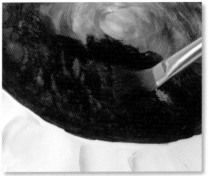

7. Brush in more chocolate brown edible food colour powder while the varnish is wet, to create a textured effect. Pat the surface with a brush to make puddles of paint.

8. While the centre is wet, pull out some of the colour to shade the central parts of the petals.

9. Cut across a size 9 round brush to create a stippling brush (see page 45) and use it to stipple round the edge of the centre, softening its edges.

10. Pick up a little bright yellow on the stippling brush and stipple part of the centre to create highlights.

11. Create a couple of accents in the centre with two sweeps of the stippling brush and bright yellow with white.

12. Pick up a mix of edible varnish, chocolate brown and food grade alcohol and flick the bristles to spatter the mix over the cake.

Opposite
Detail of the Sunflower Cake.

TOY TRAIN

All aboard this magical toy train for an introduction to the techniques required to build up a simple sugar landscape and create texture using basic household items. This adorable children's birthday cake also develops the skills you need to use simple cut-out shapes as part of an overall design. Begin by texturing the covered board using the scrubbing brush (see page 26), then edge the board with the blue ribbon. Secure the ribbon with the non-toxic glue. Place the cake in the centre of the board.

(see page 26)

1. Cut out the shapes for the sky and the ground from modelling paste using the wheel cutter and the template. Leave them to dry on a flat surface, then paint the backs with water and position the shapes on the top of the cake. Also cut a long strip of grey paste using the parallel wheel cutter or a sharp knife, paint the back with water and wrap this round the base of the cake. Trim off the ends.

You will need

25.5cm (10in) round fruit or sponge cake covered with green sugarpaste (fondant)
33cm (13in) round drum board covered with light grey sugarpaste (fondant)
Small amounts of modelling paste in pale blue, brown, grey and three shades of green
Paper template for landscape scene (page 157)
Small amounts of red, white, turquoise, purple, orange, yellow, pink and black gum paste (flower paste)
Vegetable shortening
Blue 15mm (⅝in) ribbon
Cornstarch (cornflour) dusting bag
Wheel or pizza cutter
Circle cutters, 23mm (1in), 15mm (⅝in), 11mm (½in) and 7mm (¼in)
Square cutters, 16mm (⅝in), 13mm (⅝in) and 8mm (¼in)
Square cookie cutters, 54mm (2¼in) and 35mm (1½in)
Small blossom plunger cutter
Parallel wheel cutter
Medium piping nozzle
Scrubbing brush to texture base-board icing
Smooth-blade kitchen knife
Paintbrush
Small cranked palette knife
Non-toxic glue stick
Metal ruler
Cocktail stick

2. Cut a strip of grey paste approximately 85 x 15mm (3⅜ x ⅝in) and angle the sides with a knife to make the station platform. Also cut two small grey squares using the 8mm (¼in) square cutter and a small brown square using the 16mm (⅝in) square cutter. Cut a brown square using the 35mm (1½in) cutter and cut it in half to make a rectangle.

3. For the pointed station roof, cut a black square from gum paste (flower paste) using the 16mm (⅝in) cutter and cut it in half diagonally. For the flat roof, cut a narrow black strip and angle the sides with a knife. Cut the windows, doors and clock from white paste using 7mm (¼in) circle and the 8mm (¼in) and 13mm (⅝in) square cutters. Mark the panes and the centre of the door using the edge of the knife. For the flowers, use the piping nozzle to cut tiny circles from red, pink and yellow paste.

4. Arrange all the components of the station on the front of the cake, painting the backs with water to secure them.

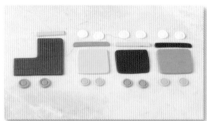

5. Cut out the components for the train. For the engine, cut a red square using the 54mm (2¼in) square cutter and remove a quarter using the same cutter. Mark on the lines using the edge of the knife. Cut out the white window using the 16mm (⅝in) square cutter, and use the same cutter to cut out the red triangular shapes for the front of the engine and the funnel.

6. Next cut three different coloured squares for the three carriages using the 35mm (1½in) square cutter, and cut four strips in different colours for the roofs. For the wheels, cut four blue and four green circles using the 15mm (⅝in) and 11mm (½in) cutters, and emboss them using the 7mm (¼in) cutter. Use the same cutter for the six white windows and emboss them in the same way.

7. Cut out three blue rectangles using the 13mm (⅝in) square cutter. Cut these in half to give rectangles for the couplings and mark on the rivets using the end of the piping nozzle. The puffs of steam are circles of white paste cut out using the 23mm (1in) and 15mm (⅝in) circle cutters, with little sections pushed in using a cocktail stick to create a scalloped edge.

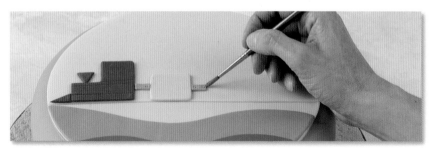

8. Attach all the train parts to the top of the cake, working left to right and sticking them in place with water painted on the backs of the shapes.

9. Once the train is in place, attach the remaining elements. Cut out some tiny coloured flowers using the small blossom plunger cutter and attach them to the grass.

10. For the tracks, cut a long brown strip approximately 25mm (1in) wide and cut off the individual sleepers using a sharp knife.

11. Secure the sleepers round the cake base. For the rails, cut two thin, grey strips using the parallel wheel cutter or a knife. Brush the sleepers with water where they will lie and place the tracks down carefully. Do this before the paste dries out so that they curve easily.

INDIAN INLAID CAKE

This beautiful cake has the look of sari fabric and is created using an inlaid design. It is important to use space bars when rolling out the sugarpaste (fondant) to cover the cake, so that the main covering and inlaid pieces are the same depth. You will also learn how to pipe with sugarpaste (fondant). Marzipan the cake and allow it to skin over before covering with sugarpaste (fondant).

You will need
17.5cm (7in) round cake, 7.5cm (3in) deep
25cm (10in) cake drum
650g (1lb 6oz) pink sugarpaste (fondant)
90g (3oz) pale jade sugarpaste (fondant)
90g (3oz) jade sugarpaste (fondant)
90g (3oz) green sugarpaste (fondant)
240g (½lb) royal icing
Edible liquid food colour (droplet) in old gold
Simple leaf cutters
Primrose cutter. 2.5cm (1in) diameter
Vodka
Scriber
Plastic side scraper
Palette knife
13mm (½in) round cutter
Piping bags size 1 and 2
Piping nozzles No.s 1, 1.5 and 2
Optional: FMM embosser (scroll set 1) for the iced cake drum
15mm (½in) satin ribbon
Non-toxic glue stick
Cash register receipt roll
Masking tape

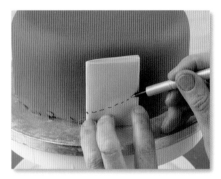

1. Take a strip of cash register receipt roll the same length as the circumference of the cake plus an extra 13mm (½in). Fold it into six equal sections (do not incorporate the extra bit). Draw then cut a scallop in the folded strip.

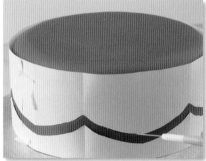

2. Unfold the length of paper and wrap both pieces round the cake leaving a 6mm (¼in) gap between the two strips. Secure the ends together with masking tape. Scribe the scallop design onto the cake. Remove the paper templates.

3. Find the central point of the curve in the scalloped design. Use the primrose cutter to cut and remove the piece of sugarpaste (fondant) from the cake covering.

4. Roll out a piece of pale jade sugarpaste (fondant) using space bars, and cut out six primrose flowers. Lightly moisten with vodka the marzipan that is now visible inside the cut-out, insert the pale jade primrose and lightly smooth the surface. Repeat to inlay all six flowers.

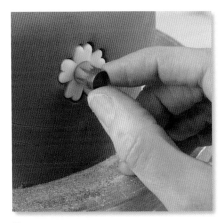 

5. Roll out a piece of jade sugarpaste (fondant) using the space bars. Use the small round cutter to cut out six discs. Use the same cutter to remove the centres from the primrose flowers and inlay the jade discs.

6. Repeat this process for the leaves and teardrop shapes.

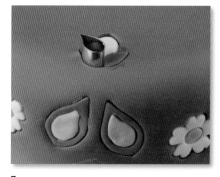

7. Cut small bud shapes from the top of the cake and inlay pale jade, with a green leaf on either side. Make sure you inlay one leaf before cutting the second out of the cake covering. Once the inlay is complete, cover the cake drum with sugarpaste (fondant) and emboss the edges. Leave the icing to skin over for twenty-four hours.

8. Tilt the cake. Overpipe the scribed scallop lines with a curved teardrop shape in old-gold-coloured royal icing, with a No. 1.5 nozzle.

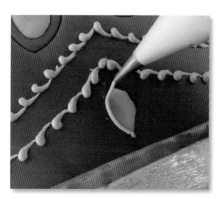

Pressure piping

By applying a steady pressure to the filled piping bag, holding it in the same place at a 90-degree angle to the surface of the icing, you can make a piped dot fatten, giving the illusion that it was created using a larger piping nozzle.

Likewise by applying a steady pressure to the filled bag while the nozzle is dragged slowly over the surface of the icing at a 35-degree angle, it can appear that it was created with a larger nozzle.

By combining these two techniques, altering the angle to 35 degrees instead of 90, you can create a teardrop with a pointed end. If the final piping action causes the piped line to snap, move the piping bag faster in relation to the amount of pressure you apply.

9. Pipe around the base teardrop inlays with a No. 1 nozzle and the same coloured royal icing.

10. Pressure pipe around the edge of the primroses with a No. 1.5 nozzle and the same coloured royal icing. Use a No. 1 nozzle and the same colour to outline the central disc.

11. Pipe a spiral on the central disc of each primrose with a No. 1 nozzle.

12. Pipe a row of evenly spaced dots between the two rows of curved teardrops with a No. 1.5 nozzle. Pipe two dots, one at the point of each scallop, then add one in the centre between them, and continue subdividing until you have a full, even decoration of dots.

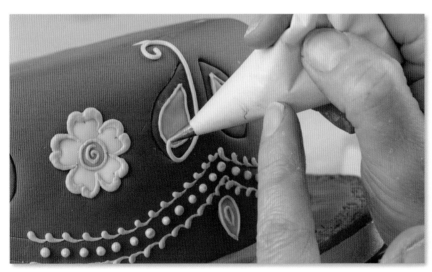

13. Outline each large leaf with No. 1.5 nozzle in a spiral design as shown, and each inner leaf with a No. 1 nozzle.

14. Outline each bud with a No. 1.5 nozzle as shown, then pipe the veins in the leaves using a No. 1 nozzle.

15. Outline the leaves with the No. 1.5 nozzle.

16 Pipe two gold teardrops using a No. 1.5 nozzle: one coming down between the large green leaves and one in the opposite direction between the top twirls.

17. Pipe five evenly spaced gold dots between the two large leaves with the No. 1 nozzle. Begin with the two end ones, pipe one centrally in between, then further subdivide with one more in each gap.

18. Pipe a small gold teardrop centrally beneath each inlaid primrose with a No. 1 nozzle. Pipe three white dots, graduating in size, on either side of the gold teardrop, using a No. 1 nozzle.

19. Pipe a white teardrop in the centre of each of the large inlaid leaves using the No. 1. nozzle. Pipe a further small white teardrop at a 45-degree angle either side of the small inlaid teardrops around the base of the cake, using the same nozzle.

20. Pipe five small white teardrops around the inlaid bud on the top edge of the cake with a No. 1 nozzle.

21. Pipe two gold teardrops either side of the small white teardrops around the base of the cake, using a No. 1 nozzle.

22. Pipe three alternating gold 'C's either side of the inlaid primroses, using a No. 1 nozzle.

23. Take a walnut-sized piece of pink sugarpaste (fondant) and dip it into a glass of water. Knead it, dip it again, then knead it a second time.

24. Transfer the piece of sugarpaste (fondant) to a plastic side scraper and continue to add water with a palette knife.

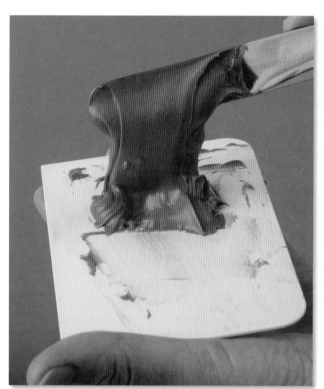

25. Paddle the sugarpaste (fondant) each time you add more water. Once the let-down sugarpaste (fondant) is soft enough to pipe with, use it to fill a size 2 piping bag with a No. 2 nozzle.

26. Pipe a snail's trail around the base of the cake with the let-down pink sugarpaste (fondant). Finish the cake by attaching a 15mm (½in) satin ribbon to the edge of the cake drum using a non-toxic glue stick.

Details of the finished cake.

FLOWER BORDER

This beautiful floral design is piped onto a cake covered in sky-blue sugarpaste (fondant), giving the impression of a glorious summer's day – perfect for a summer birthday or a keen gardener. The border design repeats three times around the cake, and you will learn how to create a template for this using cash register receipt roll. To begin, create the piped roses with pale pink royal icing and the No. 57 nozzle (see pages 28–29). Cover the cake with the blue sugarpaste (fondant), then cover the visible part of cake drum with green sugarpaste (fondant) using the bandage method (see page 20). Ideally, leave the cake covering to skin over before continuing with the decoration.

You will need
17.5cm (7in) round cake, 7.5cm (3in) deep
25cm (10in) cake drum
650g (1lb 5oz) blue sugarpaste (fondant) slightly marbled (not completely mixed)
150g (5oz) green sugarpaste (fondant)
30g (1oz) pale brown sugarpaste (fondant)
454g (1lb) royal icing
Piping nozzles No. 0, No. 1 (x 4), No.s 1.5, 2 and 57
Piping bags size 1, 2 and 3
Grass piping nozzle (Wilton 122)
Nozzle adapter
Piece of sponge for texture
30cm (12in) disposable piping bag
Edible liquid food colours (droplet): blue, buttercup, chocolate, fern green, fuchsia, grape violet, and holly green
Plastic side scraper
Palette knife
Sable paintbrush No. 2
Scriber
Scissors
Cash register receipt roll
Masking tape

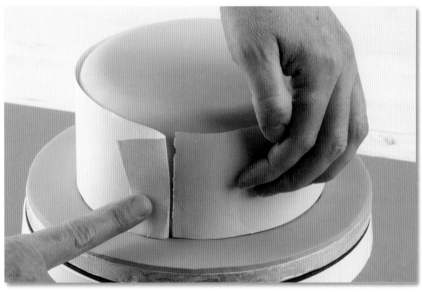

1. Divide the cake into three equal sections. The easiest way is to take a length of cash register receipt roll, wrap it around the cake and fold the end over where it meets, leaving 13mm (½in) of paper beyond the fold. Cut off the excess paper.

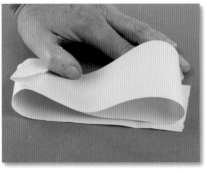

2. Fold the length of paper into three sections, not including the folded-back end. Cut out a tiny piece of paper at the base corners to mark the sections.

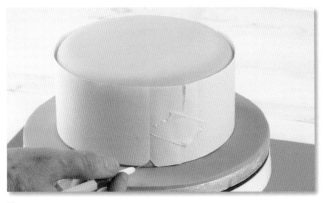

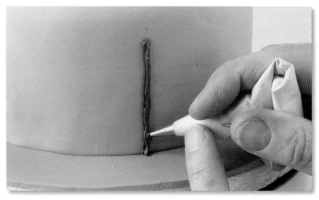

3. Wrap the strip of paper around the cake (cut-out bits to the base) and secure the ends together with masking tape. The extra 13mm (½in) is to give you an overlap i.e. to create a bit of ease should you need it. Use a scriber to mark the sections.

4. Fill a size 2 piping bag (No. 2 nozzle) with royal icing that has been coloured chocolate brown. Pipe a stem for the standard rose bush at each of the scribed marks. The stem is supposed to have an uneven finish.

5. To pipe the rose bush's leaves, create a size 3 piping bag with the tip cut for piping leaves, as shown on page 29. Half fill with royal icing coloured with a mixture of fern green and holly green liquid food colour. Use this to pipe the leaves on the standard rose bush.

6. While the leaves are still wet, attach the piped roses.

7. Next, create the lupins. Pipe the stem first using a size 1 piping bag (No. 1 nozzle) and green royal icing. Pipe the flowers with a size 2 piping bag (No. 1.5 nozzle) and violet royal icing, starting 2cm (¾in) from the base of the stem. Pipe a row of small teardrops at a slight angle, facing towards the stem, with the narrow point touching the stem. Repeat on the other side of the stem. Make three stems of lupins.

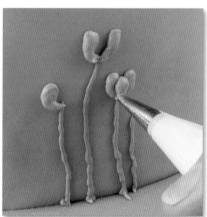

9. For the tulips, pipe the stems with a size 1 piping bag (No. 1 nozzle) and holly green royal icing. The flowers are created by piping three teardrops from a size 2 piping bag (No. 2 nozzle) and fuchsia royal icing. To create the bottom of the tulip, curve the base of the point on the first two teardrops. The central teardrops should start a fraction lower than the top of the first two teardrops.

8. Complete the lupin flowers by piping another row of teardrops on top of the green stem, finishing with a few graduated dots at the top of the stem.

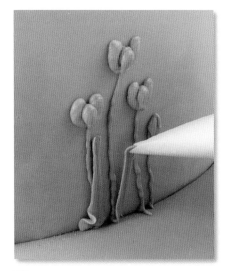

10. Add a tulip bud. Create another piping bag for piping leaves (see pages 27 and 29). Half fill it with royal icing coloured with holly green food colour. Pipe the leaves for the tulips. Starting at the base, squeeze out the royal icing to the required height, then lay it on the cake side.

11. Fill a size 1 piping bag (No. 1 nozzle) with fern green royal icing and pipe the stems for the daisies. Half fill two piping bags (No. 1 nozzles), one with white royal icing, and one with buttercup. Pipe five tiny white teardrops to create a daisy, then pipe a yellow dot in the centre.

12. Pipe green teardrops with a No. 1 nozzle to create the leaves.

13. For the yellow flowers under the standard rose bush, pipe another group of stems and leaves with the fern green royal icing, using a No. 1 nozzle. Create the flowers by piping a group of three teardrops with buttercup royal icing and the No. 1 nozzle.

69

14. Pipe a small green teardrop at the base of the yellow flower to create the calyx.

15. To create the forget-me-nots, pipe a group of long teardrops to create the leaves using a No. 1 nozzle and holly green royal icing. Pull the tip of the scriber through each leaf, base to tip, to create the midrib. Half fill a size 1 piping bag (No. 0 nozzle) with blue royal icing. Pipe a row of dots between each leaf.

16. Spread some green royal icing on the covered cake drum using the palette knife. Use a piece of sponge to create a texture. Keep turning the piece of sponge around, as if it becomes too damp, it will create spikes of royal icing rather than a fine texture.

17. Use the adapter to attach the grass nozzle to the disposable piping bag and then half fill with green royal icing. Pipe grass around the base of the cake. It is important not to touch the surface of the cake or drum with the grass nozzle, so squeeze the piping bag and let the piped lines drop onto the surface, then stop applying the pressure and then give it a quick flick (with your wrist) to snap the piped lines.

18. Create a few pebbles with the pale brown sugarpaste (fondant) and position at random on the cake drum.

MODERN BLACKWORK

This striking cake was inspired by floral tattoos and henna designs, as well as by blackwork embroidery. It features freehand piping, using a template and brush embroidery. You will also learn how to create a beautiful butterfly on acetate and transfer it to the cake top. Cover the cake with marzipan and sugarpaste (fondant) and ideally leave it to skin over before commencing any decoration.

You will need
15cm (6in) round cake, 7.5cm (3in) deep
22.5cm (9in) cake drum
Piping nozzles No.s 0, 1 and 2
Piping bags size 1 and 2 and knee-high (pop sock)
240g (8oz) of royal icing
Pure powdered food colour in black and red
2 shot glasses and 2 pipettes
Cake tilter
Edible liquid food colours (droplet) in yellow and orange
Edible petal dusts in green, red, orange and yellow
Vodka
Sable paintbrush, No. 2
Scriber
Tweezers
Artist's palette knife
Sheet of perspex (plexiglass)
Kitchen paper
Food grade acetate (butcher's wrap)
White vegetable fat
Masking tape
Small amount of sponge foam
15mm (½in) double-sided satin ribbon
Non-toxic glue stick
Black stamen cottons (optional)

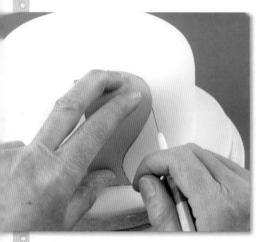

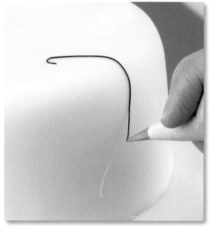

1. Divide the side of the covered cake into six equal sections. Using template A (see page 157), scribe a curved line in each section. Stop the scribed line 15mm (½in) above the base of the cake.

2. Half fill a size 1 piping bag (No. 1 nozzle) with black royal icing, made from powdered food colour. Place the cake on a tilter and pipe the scribed line, which will be a stem.

3. Freehand pipe the branches from the stem.

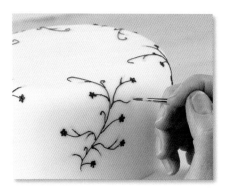

4. Using the same piping bag and nozzle, pipe five teardrops to make flowers. Mix green petal dust with a tiny amount of alcohol to create a paint. Use a fine paintbrush to paint leaves on the ends of the piped branches, freehand.

5. Once the leaves are dry, pipe an outline around them with the black royal icing and the No. 1 nozzle.

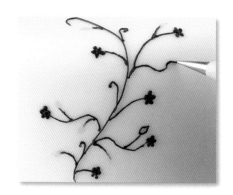

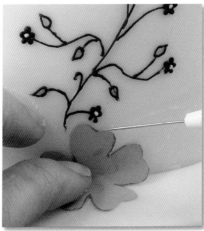

6. Half fill a size 1 piping bag (No. 1 nozzle) with yellow royal icing and pipe the centres of the small teardrop flowers. The black royal icing must be completely dry, otherwise there is a risk of the black colouring bleeding into the yellow.

7. Using a paper template made from the flower design on page 157, scribe the primrose at the base of each piped stem. Half should be on the side of the cake and the remaining half on the covered cake drum.

8. Use the various leaf templates (see page 157) to scribe leaf shapes around the primrose flowers.

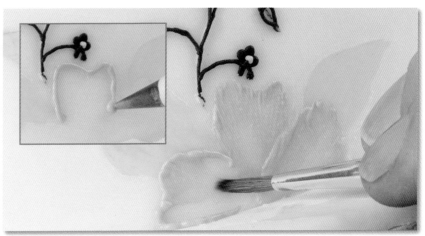

9. Paint the leaves with a mixture of green petal dust and alcohol. Scribe the next set of primrose flowers and leaves around the edge of the covered cake drum, then paint the remaining leaves.

10. Brush embroider the primrose flowers. Half fill a piping bag (No. 1 nozzle) with yellow royal icing. Pipe the outline of one of the petals (inset). Dip a No. 2 sable paintbrush in water and then remove the surplus by flattening the bristles with your index finger and thumbnail. Brush the royal icing. Start at the central point of the edge of the petal and then fan the brush strokes from the outside edge to the flower centre. The brush movement must stop at the centre of the flower and not before – even if you think there is no royal icing on the brush. This will ensure a shaded petal is created and not a petal with a royal icing outline. Outline one petal at a time and then brush it before outlining the next, or the royal icing will have dried before you have a chance to brush it. If the brush is too dry, it will pull the royal icing off the surface of the cake, but if it is too wet, there will be no brush strokes visible on the petals.

11. Half fill a piping bag (No. 0 nozzle) with black royal icing. Scratch pipe a central line down each large leaf by dragging the nozzle in the cake surface as you pipe. Pipe the veins from the central line to the leaf edge. Re-pipe the central vein of the leaves. Pressure pipe the outline of the leaves using a No. 1 piping nozzle.

12. Pressure pipe the outline of the primrose flower with black royal icing and a No. 1 nozzle. Pipe the centres of the primrose flowers with black royal icing and a No. 0 nozzle.

13. Fill some of the open spaces around the primrose flowers with stretched teardrop shapes.

14. Fill some of the remaining open spaces with freehand piped spirals – these look more effective if they are pressure piped, but you might find it easier to pipe the spiral with a No. 0 nozzle first and then pressure pipe over this shape with a No. 1 nozzle.

15. Finish the primrose flowers by piping three tiny lines on each petal of the flower.

16. Secure a piece of food grade acetate or wax paper to a sheet of perspex (plexiglass) or a flat board, with a few pieces of masking tape. Apply a tiny amount of white vegetable fat to the acetate and then wipe it off. Take a clean piece of kitchen paper and wipe the surface of the acetate again. If there is too much fat on the surface, it will break down the royal icing. Slide the butterfly template (see page 157) under the piece of acetate. Half fill a piping bag (No. 2 nozzle) with white royal icing. Pipe a small amount of royal icing at the base of each wing and then brush it, fanning out the brush strokes from the base of the wing. Create the same shape as the outline on the template. Complete all four wings.

17. Once the wings are dry, paint them with petal dust mixed with alcohol. Use yellow close to the body, radiating out to orange and then red at the tips.

18. Pipe the details on the wings with black royal icing and the No. 0 piping nozzle.

19. Complete all the wings.

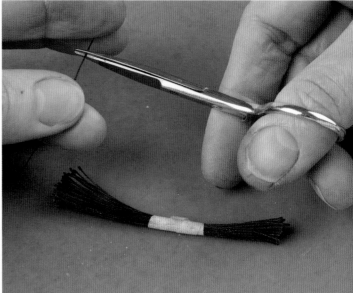

20. Creating the antennae of the butterflies is optional. If you opt to use the stamen cottons, then this item needs to be classed as non-edible and must be removed before the cake is cut. Cut a stamen cotton in half.

21. Pipe a body for the butterfly on top of the cake with black royal icing and a No. 2 nozzle. Use the artist's palette knife to release the butterfly wings from the acetate. Insert a tiny amount of each wing into the freshly piped body. Place a tiny piece of sponge foam under each wing to create a more lifelike pose.

22. If you are using them, insert two stamen cottons into the head of the butterfly to create the antennae. Once dry, the sponge supports can be removed.To finish the cake, attach a 15mm (½in) satin ribbon to the edge of the cake drum using a non-toxic glue stick.

Details of the finished cake.

POPPY CAKE

Poppies are always a favourite flower to paint on a cake, and the bright, vibrant colours against white icing create stunning results. This design is popular with all ages. Finish it off with a decorative border punched out of sugar sheet with a craft border punch, and a flamboyant ribbon with an added bow. To decorate the bow, push in three green leaf hat pins. Trim the cake board with green ribbon.

1. Paint the top petals of the main poppy flowers as you would a scalloped leaf (see page 43), with the 10mm (⅜in) brush loaded with cherry red and burgundy. The darker burgundy should go towards the centres.

2. Paint the side and lower petals in the same way.

3. Paint the buds with little flat leaf shapes, with the burgundy at the top.

4. Without cleaning the brush, pick up dark green and white and paint the main stems (see page 48). Again, without cleaning the brush, use citrus green and white to paint the stems to the buds.

5. Paint poppy leaves with dark green and citrus green, following the instructions on page 44.

6. Complete the second side of the poppy leaf.

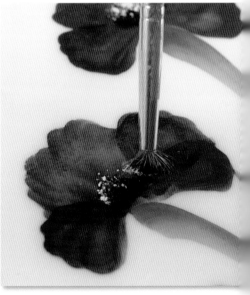

7. Use a size 5 round brush cut for stippling (see page 45) to stipple the black poppy centres in the main flowers.

8. Pick up dry grains of yellow edible powder food colour and stipple them on to create pollen in the poppy centres. Add small filler leaves in dark green and white with the 6mm (¼in) flat brush.

Opposite
Detail from the Poppy Cake.

CHOCOLATE HEART

I love the contrast between the covered milk chocolate cake and the dark chocolate embossed stencilling. It is simple yet dramatic. The technique is very quick, and that makes this cake perfect when time is of the essence.

You will need

Budding Heart stencil
20cm (8in) heart-shaped cake covered with chocolate sugarpaste (fondant)
Palette knife and dark chocolate
Large plate and white vegetable fat

1. Rub a thin layer of white vegetable fat over the back of the stencil and place it on top of the chocolate sugarpaste (fondant)-covered cake. Warm some chocolate, then temper the chocolate on a large plate. When the chocolate holds the lines you make with the palette knife, it is ready to apply.

2. Quickly pour a relatively small amount of chocolate on to the top of the stencil.

Tip

If the chocolate sets too quickly, warm the surface gently with a hairdryer.

3. Working quickly, use your palette knife to spread the chocolate as thinly and smoothly as you can over the surface.

4. Before the chocolate sets, peel away the stencil to reveal the finished cake.

The finished Chocolate Heart cake, along with a smaller cake made in the same way. Both have had matching gold and white ribbons added.

HOT-AIR BALLOONS

This uplifting design uses cutters and embellishers to create a summer landscape complete with clouds and balloons. Icing the decorations onto lollipop sticks lifts the decorative scene and gives height to the design. Begin by securing the ribbon round the cake base using the non-toxic glue and placing the cake in the centre of the board.

You will need

15cm (6in) round fruit or sponge cake, 13cm (5in) deep, covered with pale blue sugarpaste (fondant)
20.5cm (8in) round drum board covered with green sugarpaste (fondant)
Small amounts of dark and mid green, white, yellow, orange, red, fuchsia pink, purple and light brown modelling paste
Small amounts of mid brown gum paste (flower paste)
Vegetable shortening
Purple 15mm (⅝in) ribbon
Cornstarch (cornflour) dusting bag
Parallel wheel cutter
Wheel or pizza cutter
Round cookie cutters, 85mm (3⅜in), 65mm (2½in) and 50mm (2in)
Rectangular cutters, 25 x 14mm (1 x ⅝in) and 20 x 11mm (¾ x ½in)
Rose petal cutters, 63mm (2½in) and 54mm (2¼in) long
Small blossom plunger cutters, 13mm (⅝in) and 10mm (½in)
Stitching wheel
Piping bag and fine piping nozzle
Lollipop sticks
Smooth-blade kitchen knife
Paintbrush
Royal icing
Small cranked palette knife
Non-toxic glue stick

1. Cut a strip of mid green paste using the parallel wheel cutter, long enough to fit round the base of the cake. Create a wavy edge on one side using a wheel cutter or pizza cutter. Attach the strip to the base of the cake and trim off the excess. Apply water to the cake first so that the paste sticks.

2. Make four or five clouds in several sizes (see page 22). Also cut ten or more different-sized flower shapes from dark green paste using the blossom cutters, then cut ten more from the mid green paste and cut them in half for the shrubs. The tree trunks are brown rectangles cut with a knife.

3. For each balloon, make five small balls of paste and roll them into approximately 6cm (2¼in) lengths, tapered at each end.

4. Place them in the right order, then coat the inner sides with water and push them together. Squeeze the ends to make a balloon shape.

5. Use a rose petal cutter to cut out the balloon. Make six or seven all together, using two different sizes of rose petal cutter.

6. Use the stitching wheel to mark a stitch line along some of the stripes (there's no need to mark all of them).

7. Trim off the base of the balloon with a knife. For the basket, cut a mid brown rectangle of gum paste (flower paste) using the larger of the two rectangular cutters, then cut a smaller rectangle from one side using the smaller cutter.

8. Emboss the basket using a knife.

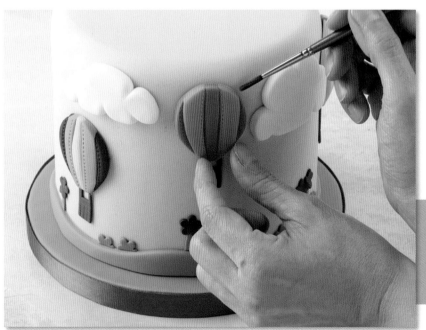

9. Attach the light elements to the side of the cake using water applied to the back of each shape with a paintbrush. Attach the heavier elements such as the clouds and balloons with royal icing either brushed or piped onto the back of the items for a secure fix. Retain three clouds and three balloons for decorating the top of the cake.

Tip

If you need to reposition a shape, don't try to remove it – simply slide it into its new position.

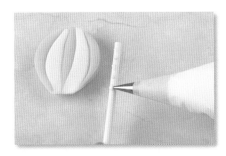

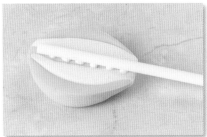

10. For each of the balloons on the top of the cake, pipe small dots of royal icing along the top of a lollipop stick.

11. Press the lollipop stick firmly to the back of the balloon, making sure it is straight. Allow to dry for several hours for a firm bond.

12. Pipe a tiny dot of icing on the back of the basket and attach it just below the balloon.

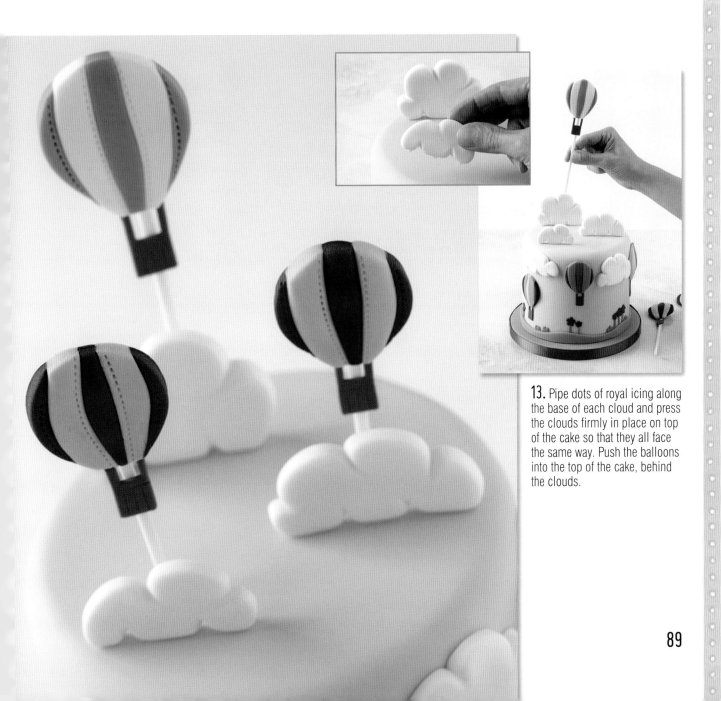

13. Pipe dots of royal icing along the base of each cloud and press the clouds firmly in place on top of the cake so that they all face the same way. Push the balloons into the top of the cake, behind the clouds.

ROSE BASKET

In this project you will learn how to make marzipan roses, spilling out of a basket made from a royal-icing-coated cake. There are various possibilities with basketweave designs. The rose basket is made with the classic technique, using a flat serrated nozzle and a plain round nozzle. A few more styles of basketweave are shown at the end of this project in case you are inspired to branch out.

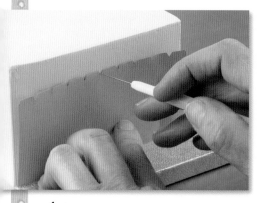

1. Create a paper template the same size as one side of the cake and divide it into an even number of sections approximately 13mm (½in) apart. Use a scriber to mark these sections onto the side of the cake.

2. Use a set square to scribe vertical lines on the cake sides to create the sections. Coat the cake drum with royal icing (see pages 18–19). Leave to dry for eight hours. Place a No. 22 basketweave nozzle in a large piping bag (size 4). Paddle a quantity of cream-coloured royal icing on the work surface and half fill the piping bag. Place a No. 3 nozzle in a size 3 piping bag. Half fill the piping bag with royal icing coloured brown.

3. Place the cake on a cake tilter. Using the No. 3 nozzle, pipe a line directly on top of one of the scribed lines (start at the top edge of the cake and finish at the base). If necessary, use a damp paintbrush to correct the line and neaten the take-off point. Starting at the top edge of the cake, pipe a short horizontal line using the No. 22 nozzle from the scribed line before the vertical piped line to the scribed line after it. Leave a gap the width of the nozzle and repeat down the side of the cake.

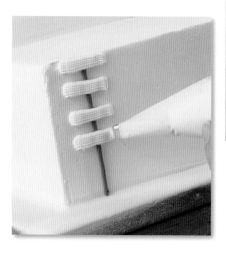

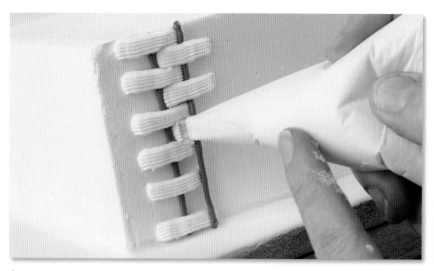

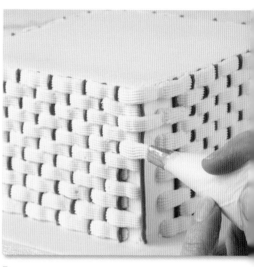

4. Pipe another brown vertical line with the No. 3 nozzle on the next scribed line, to the right of the previous vertical line and going over the No. 22 horizontal piped lines. Using the No. 22 nozzle, pipe a short horizontal line in the gap, starting at the side of the first brown vertical line and lifting it over the second. Finish at the scribed line to the right of the brown vertical line.

5. Repeat until the cake sides are completely piped.

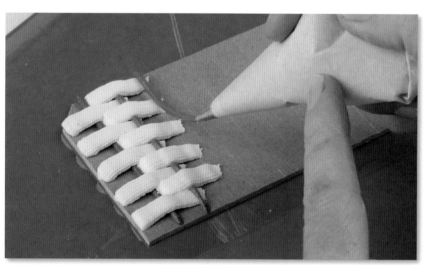

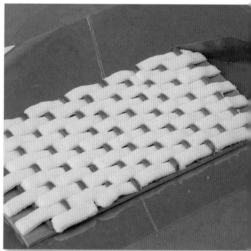

6. Take a cake board the same size as the top of the cake and cut it in half. Cut across the two top corners. Scribe vertical lines on the underside (not the silver side). Pipe a basketweave design for the basket lid.

7. Clean up the edges of the lid if necessary using an artist's palette knife. Leave to dry.

8. Divide the cake top into two equal portions using the scriber and a ruler.

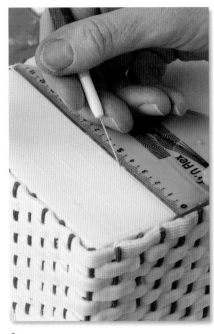
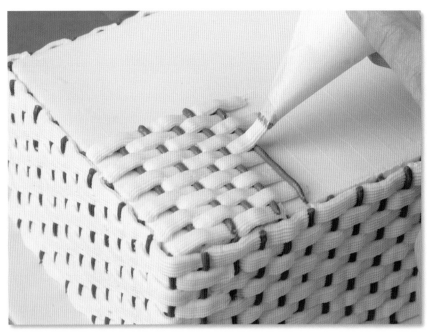

9. Scribe vertical lines in the same way as on the cake sides, on one half of the top.

10. Pipe a basketweave as before over half the cake top.

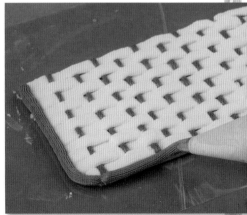

11. Place a No. 43 nozzle in a size 3 piping bag. Half fill the piping bag with royal icing, coloured brown. Pipe a line around the top edge of the cake, half on the top and half on the side, to hide the join. Leave to dry.

12. Place the basket lid on a piece of food grade acetate and pipe a line in the same way around three sides. Leave to dry for no less than four hours.

MAKING MARZIPAN ROSES

These are pulled roses – in other words they are produced without using a cutter. While the icing is drying, create the marzipan roses and leaves. Colour the marzipan with fuchsia paste food colour.

Tip

When working with marzipan, it is easier if you keep a film of water on your hands. Keep wiping your hands on a damp cloth. No glue is required, as marzipan sticks to itself.

13. Take a walnut-sized piece of marzipan and roll it into a ball and then a cone. Place six small balls of marzipan 13mm (½in) across, in a good quality plastic food bag. Use your thumb to flatten them. Thin the top edge with your index finger, leaving the base of the petal thick. When removing the flattened balls from the bag, pick them up by their thickest edge.

 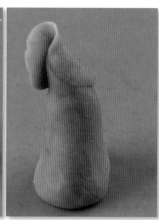

14. Position the first petal 3mm (⅛in) above the tip of the cone. Tightly wrap the first petal around the cone, one side at a time.

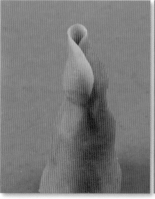 

15. When looking down on to this first petal, you should not be able to see the tip of the cone shape. Attach a further two petals to the cone, interleaving them – the right-hand side of the front petal should be tucked in first.

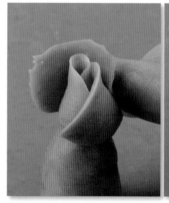

16. Attach a further three petals to the cone, interleaving as before.

17. For a larger rose, make five more petals and attach them to the cone, again interleaving them.Gently press the cone with your index fingers and thumbs where the last petals were attached, to create a rounded base of the rose. Cut the rose from the cone.

MAKING MARZIPAN LEAVES

Colour the marzipan with spruce green paste food colour for these pulled leaves.

The finished marzipan rose and leaf.

18. Take a large pea-sized piece of marzipan and roll it into a ball and then a double-ended cone. Place it in a plastic food bag and use your thumb to flatten it. Thin the side edges with your index finger. Remove the leaf from the bag, pinch it to make a central vein and then place it on a piece of crumpled foil to firm up.

COMPLETING THE BASKET

19. Place a No. 1 nozzle in a small piping bag (size 2). Take sufficient royal icing (coloured brown) to half fill the piping bag. Paddle on a side scraper and then sieve using a knee-high (see page 8) and fill the piping bag. Pipe lines over the brown basket edging at a 45-degree angle, keeping the lines as close as possible.

20. Secure the marzipan roses and leaves to the top of the cake using cream-coloured royal icing.

21. Keep checking (with the lid) that you have not over-filled the top of the cake with the marzipan roses and leaves.

22. Once you are happy that you have enough roses and leaves, pipe a line of cream-coloured royal icing and secure the basket lid. Use a damp paintbrush to neaten the join.

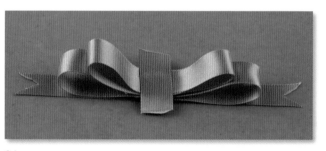

23. Make a double flat bow. Cut four lengths of ribbon: 14cm (5½in), 23cm (9in), 17.8cm (7in) and 3cm (1¼in). Place a small piece of double-sided sticky tape on one end of the 23cm (9in) length and attach the opposite end to make a loop. Repeat with the 17.8cm (7in) length. Place a piece of the tape inside each loop at the join, ensure that the join is central and press the loop to create a figure '8'. Repeat with the smaller loop. Secure the larger loop centrally on the 14cm (5½in) strip of ribbon. Place another piece of double-sided tape centrally on the 23cm (9in) loop and attach the 17.8cm (7in) loop.

24. Attach a small piece of double-sided tape at the central point on the loops and secure the last piece of ribbon. Wrap this small piece round the bow and secure with tape at the back.

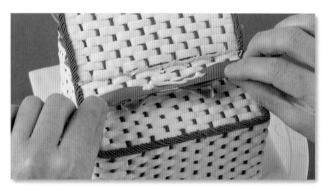

25. Secure the bow to the cake with cream-coloured royal icing. To finish the cake, attach a 13mm (½in) satin ribbon to the edge of the cake drum using non-toxic glue stick. Overlap the ribbon at the back of the cake by 13mm (½in).

A detail of the finished cake.

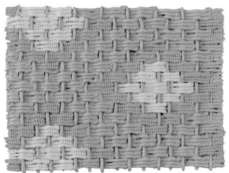

Further examples of basketweave designs that you can make with piping.

SCROLLS AND ROSES

This lavishly decorated cake would be perfect for an important wedding anniversary. You will learn how to create a gorgeous effect with scrolls and how to pipe intricate graduated linework. Make the piped roses using yellow royal icing and a No. 57 nozzle (see pages 28–29). It is optional to catch the edges of the dried roses with burgundy petal dust. Coat the cake and cake drum with royal icing.

<table>
<tr><td colspan="1">You will need</td></tr>
<tr><td>15cm (6in) round cake, 10cm (4in) deep</td></tr>
<tr><td>22.5cm (9in) cake drum</td></tr>
<tr><td>Piping nozzles No.s 1, 2, 3, 43, 44 and 57</td></tr>
<tr><td>Piping bags size 1, 2, 3, and 4</td></tr>
<tr><td>Scissors</td></tr>
<tr><td>Scriber</td></tr>
<tr><td>Cake tilter</td></tr>
<tr><td>Scalpel and cutting mat or sticky notes</td></tr>
<tr><td>Sable paintbrush No. 2</td></tr>
<tr><td>Edible liquid food colours (droplet) in buttercup and fern green</td></tr>
<tr><td>Burgundy edible petal dust</td></tr>
<tr><td>900g (2lb) white royal icing</td></tr>
<tr><td>13mm (½in) double satin ribbon</td></tr>
<tr><td>Non-toxic glue stick</td></tr>
</table>

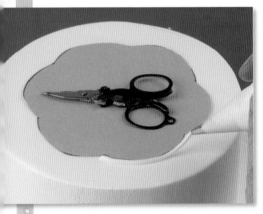

1. Create the template for the top of the cake from the design on page 158. Place it centrally with a small weighted item on top to hold it in place. Half fill a size 3 piping bag (No. 3 nozzle) with white royal icing. Pipe a line as close to the template as possible without touching. Stop and restart the line at every point.

2. Use a damp paintbrush if necessary to tidy or sharpen the joins.

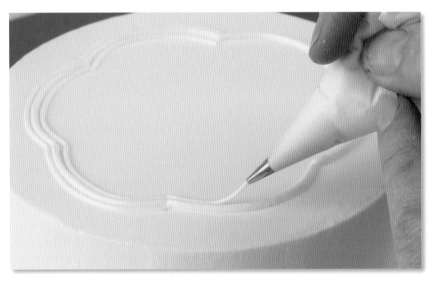

3. Carefully remove the template. Half fill a size 2 piping bag (No. 2 nozzle) with white royal icing. Pipe a line either side of the first line. These lines need to be as close as possible without touching. Stop and restart the line at every point. Use a damp paintbrush as before to tidy or sharpen the joins.

4. Using the same piping bag and nozzle, pipe a line directly on top of the first line (the one you did with the No. 3 nozzle). Use a damp paintbrush if necessary.

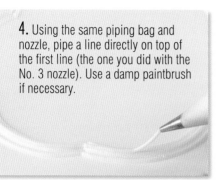

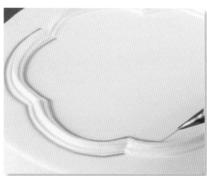

5. Half fill a size 2 piping bag (No. 1 nozzle) with green royal icing. Pipe a green line either side of the outer white No. 2 nozzle lines. Make sure the green lines are as close as possible without touching. Stop and restart the line at every point and use a paintbrush as before if needed.

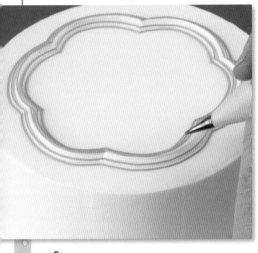

6. Overpipe the other piped white lines with the green royal icing.

7. Divide the top edge of the cake into six sections with a dot of royal icing, using the No. 2 nozzle. These sections should line up with points on the piped design. Half fill a size 4 piping bag (No. 44 nozzle) with white royal icing. You can pipe agitated or rope scrolls, but be consistent throughout the cake. Those shown are agitated scrolls. The scroll needs to start on the top of the cake (at the dot), move down on to the cake side, then finish on the top at the next dot. The scrolls on this cake are alternating (mirror image): the first scrolls starts from the left and goes anticlockwise (to the right), and the next scroll starts on the right and goes clockwise (to the left).

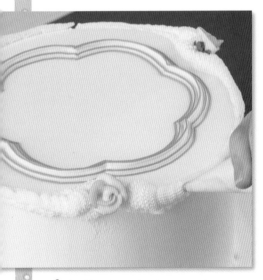

8. Position three piped roses on the top edge of the cake while the royal icing is still soft. Half fill a size 4 piping bag (No. 43 nozzle) with white royal icing. Overpipe the alternating scrolls.

9. Pipe another set of alternating scrolls (No. 43 nozzle) on the top of the cake: start at the centre of a scallop's curve and finish at the same point as the first set of alternating scrolls.

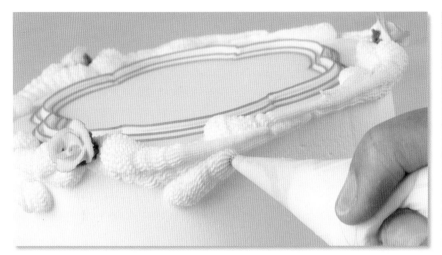

10. Pipe another set of alternating scrolls on the side of the cake, starting halfway between the first and second scroll and finishing at the same point as the first set of alternating scrolls.

11. Divide the base of the cake into six sections with a dot of royal icing (No. 2 nozzle). These sections should line up with the previous dots. Pipe alternating scrolls between the dots, with a No.44 nozzle.

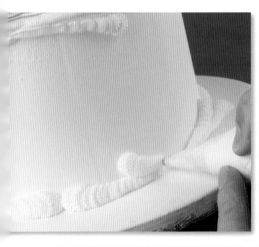

12. Pipe the additional alternating scrolls along the base with the No. 43 nozzle.

13. Attach the piped roses along the base while the royal icing is still soft.

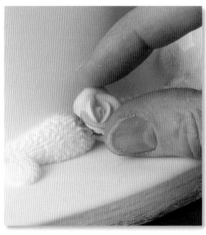

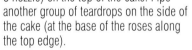

14. Pipe a group of five teardrops (No. 3 nozzle) on the top of the cake. Pipe another group of teardrops on the side of the cake (at the base of the roses along the top edge).

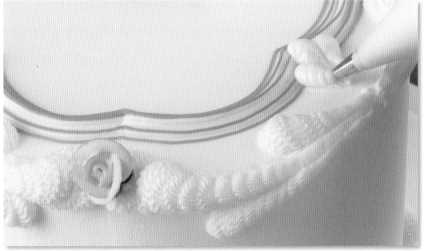

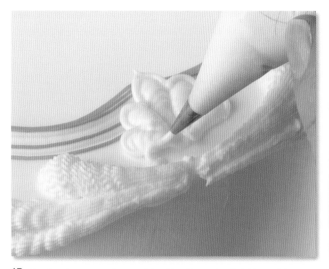

15. Outline these teardrops with a No. 2 nozzle, finishing with two alternating 'C's.

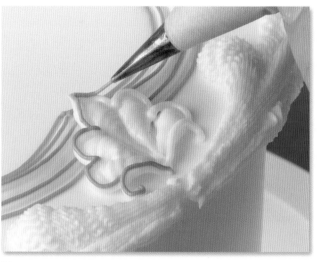

16. Overpipe the No. 2 white line with green royal icing, using the No. 1 nozzle.

17. Overpipe the white alternating scrolls with a No. 3 nozzle and white royal icing.

18. Overpipe the No. 3 lines in white with a No. 2 nozzle.

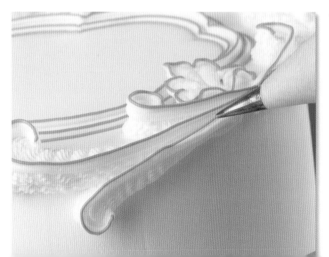

19. Overpipe the No. 2. white lines with green royal icing using a No. 1 nozzle.

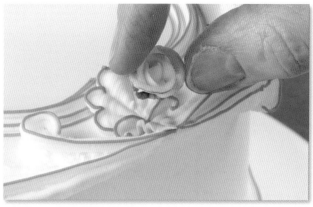

20. Create a piping bag for piping leaves (see pages 27 and 29). Half fill with green royal icing. Pipe a leaf at the base of each group of No. 3 teardrops on the top of the cake.

21. Attach the piped roses while the royal icing is still soft.

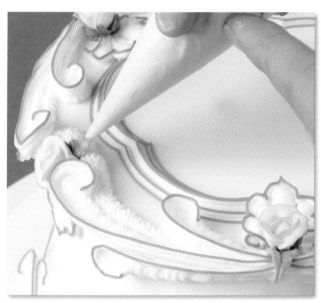

23. Pipe three leaves around the other roses along the top edge.

22. Pipe another leaf at the back of each rose.

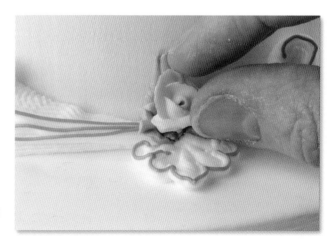

24. Pipe a group of three leaves, then attach a rose where each group of teardrops at the base of the cake is piped.

25. Copy the template on page 158. Place it on a cutting mat or a block of sticky notes and carefully cut along the lines using a scalpel. Secure the template to the side of the cake with a few dots of royal icing. Carefully scribe the design onto the side of the cake.

26. Tilt the cake and overpipe the scribed lines with a No. 2 nozzle and white royal icing. Pipe a group of three teardrops centrally at the base of the design. Overpipe the teardrops with a No. 2 nozzle.

27. Pipe three green dots (No. 2 nozzle) graduating in size at the centre of the design. Pipe two alternating teardrops at either side of the design. Overpipe the No. 2 lines in green royal icing with a No. 1 nozzle.

28. Half fill a size 2 piping bag (No. 2 nozzle) with buttercup royal icing and pipe the final group of dots and a teardrop below as shown. To finish the cake, attach a 13mm (½in) satin ribbon to the edge of the cake drum with non-toxic glue stick, overlapping at the back of the cake by 13mm (½in).

Details from the finished cake. Once the piped roses are fully dry, dry dust with burgundy edible petal dust.

TRELLIS CAKE

This project shows how stylish using buttercream can be through a larger stencil. The same stencil has been used on the ribbon embellishment to create a sophisticated look.

You will need

30cm (12in) and 20cm (8in) *Large Decorative Trellis* stencils
30cm (12in) and 20cm (8in) square cakes, both covered with lilac sugarpaste (fondant)
15mm (⅝in) flat brush
Edible dusting powder in metallic purple
Palette knife and kitchen knife
Ivory sugarpaste (fondant), rolling pin and spacers
Buttercream
30mm (1⅛in) circle cutters
White vegetable fat and edible glue
Pins

1. Put the smaller cake on top of the larger. Pin the 30cm (12in) stencil to the side of the larger cake and use the palette knife to apply buttercream to each side in turn. Repeat the process on the smaller cake with the 20cm (8in) stencil.

2. Cover the surface with white fat and roll out ivory sugarpaste (fondant) into a long strip. Use the rolling pin to emboss the surface with the 30cm (12in) stencil. Use the very large flat brush to apply metallic purple edible dusting powder. Remove the stencil and make a second piece in the same way.

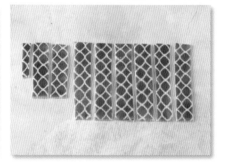

3. Use a sharp kitchen knife to trim away any excess sugarpaste (fondant) so you have two wide pieces completely covered by the pattern. Next, cut the pieces into the following smaller strips: six 13 x 2.5cm (5⅛ x 1in); two 9 x 2.5cm (3½ x 1in); and one 5 x 1.5cm (2 x ½in).

4. Carefully wrap one of the 13cm (5⅛in) strips around the 30mm (1⅛in) circle cutter. Apply a little edible glue to glue the ends together, then use a sharp knife to cut away any excess icing and to trim away the corners of the fused piece.

5. Repeat the process for the remaining five 13cm (5⅛in) strips and leave them to dry for an hour. While you wait, curl the smallest strip into a horseshoe shape and trim the ends, then drape the two longer strips over 30mm (1⅛in) circle cutters and cut the ends as shown.

6. Arrange five of the prepared loops in the centre of the top of the cake and then slip one of the longer strips into the space. Place the second long strip over the first, and use a sharp knife to trim away where they overlap.

7. Set the final loop in place over the two longer strips, then add the tiny loop in the centre.

CAMEO CAKE

Cameos are always a favourite and look stunning layered on to different colours of icing in this timeless wedding cake project. This project also shows you how to stencil directly on to the cake using a large stencil, and how to fill in areas that the stencil can not reach in one go.

You will need

Cameo and *Filigree Swirl* stencils

30cm (12in), 25.5cm (10in) and 20cm (8in), round cakes, all covered with white sugarpaste (fondant)

Edible dusting powders in light blue and silver

Sugarpaste in white and baby blue

Organza ribbon in shades of light blue

Buttercream coloured blue

Icing bag with a round nozzle

Cutters: large and medium double-sided oval

Royal icing

15mm (⅝in) flat brush

Palette knife

Pins and string

Edible pearls

White vegetable fat

Edible glue

1. Wrap the *Filigree Swirl* stencil all the way round the 30cm (12in) cake and pin it in place. If your stencil does not reach, then take a piece of string and cut a length equal to the gap between the pattern – note that this is not the ends of the stencil. Put the piece of string to one side.

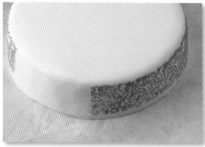

2. Cover the stencil with buttercream following the instructions on page 37, but substituting the chocolate with blue buttercream. Carefully remove the stencil, wash it clean and let it dry.

3. Use your scissors to cut a length of the stencil equal to the length of the string from step 1. Ensure you do not keep any of the outside border. Pin this piece in the gap, following the instructions for pattern matching on pages 40–41.

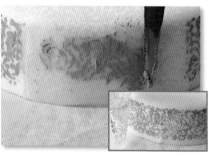

4. Secure the stencil in place with blue buttercream in the centre, remove the pins and cover the rest of the border. Once dry, carefully remove the stencil (see inset).

5. Roll out a small amount of white sugarpaste (fondant) to a thickness of 3mm (⅛in). Place the cameo stencil on top. Use a 15mm (⅝in) flat brush to dust the whole stencil area with light blue dusting powder, then pick up a little silver on the same brush and lightly dust the portrait.

The finished Cameo Cake would be perfect for a wedding.

6. Use the oval side of the double-sided cutter to cut round the portrait.

7. Prepare and roll out some baby blue sugarpaste (fondant), then use the scalloped side of the double-sided cutter to cut out a scalloped oval. Pick up the portrait oval on your palette knife and place it carefully on top of the scalloped oval. Make five more of these and leave them to dry.

8. Cut out an oval from white sugarpaste (fondant) using the large double-sided cutter, and put one of the five assembled pieces on top. Turn over the cutter and cut out a large scalloped oval from baby blue sugarpaste (fondant) and place the assembled piece on top to complete the cameo. Make five more of these for a total of eleven cameos (five with one layer of backing and six larger ones with three layers of backing).

9. Place the 25.5cm (10in) and 20cm (8in) cakes on top of the larger cake. Wrap the bottom of each new layer with light blue organza ribbon, then wrap slightly mid-blue ribbon over the top of the light blue ribbons.

10. Secure one of the larger cameos to the middle tier of the cake using edible glue.

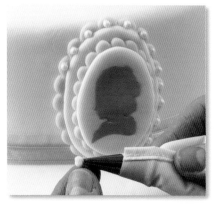

11. Take an icing bag with a round nozzle and fill it with royal icing. Use a tiny dab of icing to attach an edible pearl into each scallop of the background layer.

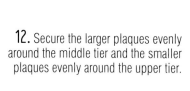

12. Secure the larger plaques evenly around the middle tier and the smaller plaques evenly around the upper tier.

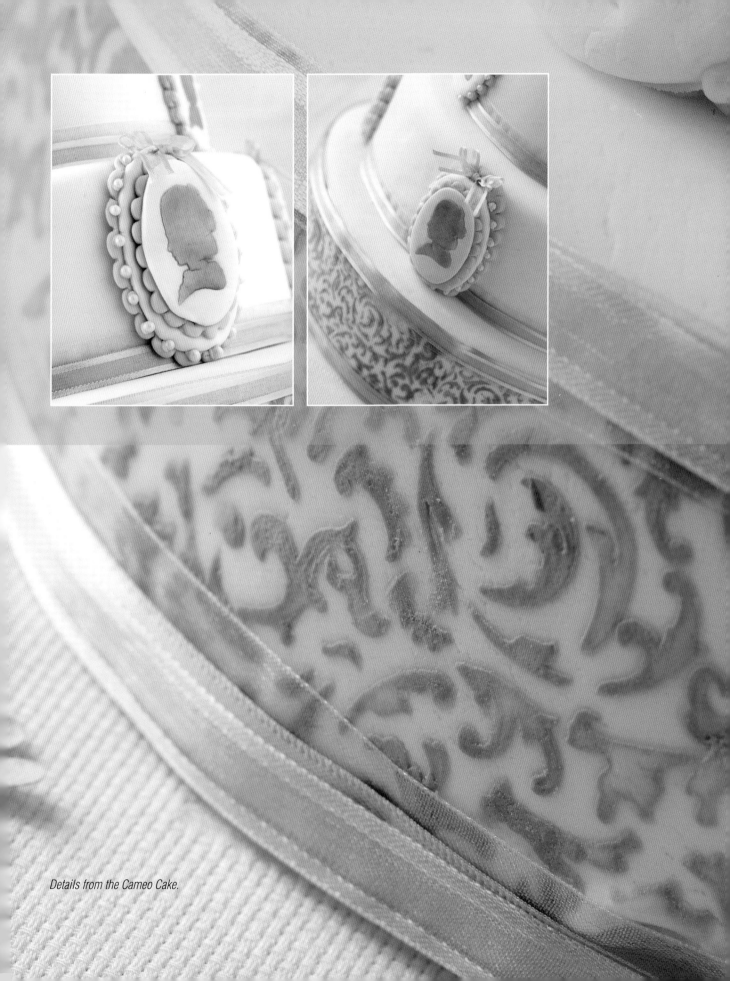

Details from the Cameo Cake.

ENGAGEMENT HEART

This romantic cake has a traditional feel even though it is covered with sugarpaste (fondant) rather than royal icing. It is then piped with a delicate flower design in subtle colours. You will learn how to create a template for the cake sides to help you to pipe the scalloped design. Marzipan the cake before covering it with white sugarpaste (fondant). Cover the cake drum with the same. If possible, allow the covering to skin over before continuing.

1. Make a paper template for the side of the cake. Take a strip of cash register receipt roll the same length as the cake plus 13mm (½in). Divide and fold it into five equal sections, without incorporating the extra bit. Fold the folded paper in half again and draw then cut a half scallop. Unfold the length of paper and wrap it round the cake. Secure the ends together with a piece of masking tape. The extra bit is to give you an overlap i.e. create a bit of ease. Place a small bottle or something similar between the lobes of the heart to keep the template in place.

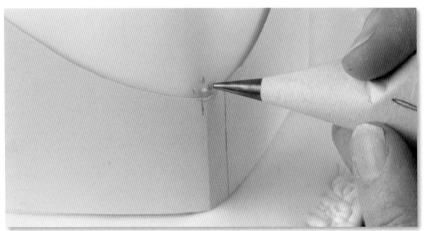

Tip

Work on the piping details for all five sections at the same time, to keep each piped section even in size.

2. Half fill a size 1 piping bag (No. 1 nozzle) with buttercup-coloured royal icing. Using the paper template as a guide, pipe a tiny yellow dot at the central point on each of the scallops. Be careful not to pipe on the paper template. Half fill a size 1 piping bag (No. 1 nozzle) with fuchsia-coloured royal icing. Pipe half of the flower (three tiny teardrops) around the yellow dot. Ensure the piped petals do not touch the central dot.

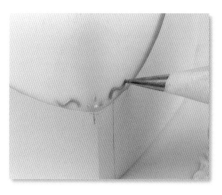

3. Half fill a size 1 piping bag (No. 1 nozzle) with green-coloured royal icing. Pipe a small wavy line either side of the flower, keeping them even in size.

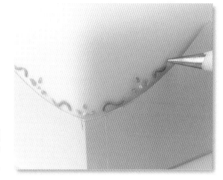

4. Pipe another half flower (yellow dot and three teardrops) either side of the wavy lines, then add more wavy lines as shown.

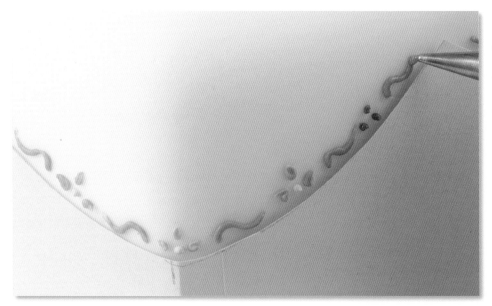

5. Half fill a size 1 piping bag (No. 0 nozzle) with grape violet-coloured royal icing. Don't forget to use a knee-high to sieve the royal icing. Pipe a group of three dots. Finish with another wavy line.

6. Remove the paper template and complete the side design by finishing off the flowers, and piping the final wavy line. Pipe small teardrops for leaves either side of each wavy green line.

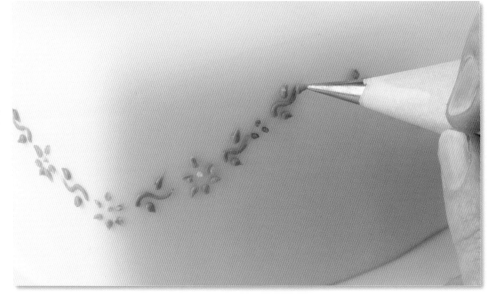

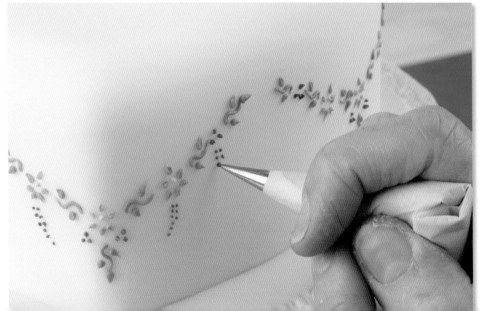

7. Use the size 1 piping bag (No. 0 nozzle) with grape violet-coloured royal icing to pipe curved clusters of dots, suggesting hanging blossoms. Ensure the shapes curve towards the centre of the design.

8. Transfer the heart template on page 158 onto paper and place it centrally on top of the cake. Use a scriber to transfer the basic shape by pin-pricking the centre of each flower and one of each of the groups of three dots. Remove the paper template.

9. Pipe a tiny dot of buttercup royal icing on top of each flower pin prick. Pipe a group of three grape-violet-coloured dots at the other pin prick marks.

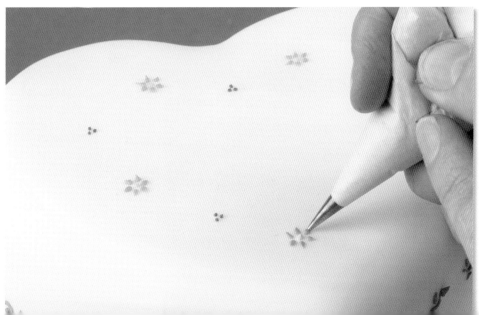

10. Pipe six tiny pale pink teardrops around each of the yellow dots, without touching the dots, to create flowers.

11. Pipe a small green wavy line between the piped flowers and the groups of three dots.

12. Pipe two small teardrops for leaves, one each side of each wavy line. Half fill a size 2 piping bag (No. 2 nozzle) with white royal icing. Freehand pipe the Inscription in the centre of the heart and then overpipe in a colour of your choice, using a No. 1 nozzle.

Piping letters freehand

It is always a good idea to practise piping the required letters on the work surface first; this allows you to get an idea of the size and a feel for the movement which will be required. Do not drag the nozzle over the surface – allow the piped line to drop onto the surface. If necessary, a small amount of correction of the letter shape can be made with a damp paintbrush.

13. Pipe a snail's trail around the base of the cake with the same nozzle and white royal icing.To finish, attach a 15mm (½in) satin ribbon to the edge of the cake drum using a non-toxic glue stick.

Details of the finished cake.

WEDDING CAKE

This romantic wedding cake has been given a contemporary twist with its single deep tier. The stylized sugar flowers make an eye-catching statement and the colours can be adapted to match any wedding theme. Decorative borders and sugar buttons add style, and sugar pearls and lustre effects complete the look. Begin by edging the board with peach ribbon, securing it using non-toxic glue, then stack the cake using cake dowels.

You will need

10cm (4in), 20.5cm (8in) and 25.5cm (10in) round fruit or sponge cakes, each 7.5cm (3in) deep, placed on same-size hard boards and covered with ivory sugarpaste (fondant)
15cm (6in) round fruit or sponge cake, 15cm (6in) deep, placed on same-size hard board and covered with ivory sugarpaste (fondant)
30.5cm (12in) round drum board covered with ivory sugarpaste (fondant)
Cake dowels to support tiers
Small amounts of gum paste (flower paste) in three different shades of peach
Pearl lustre powder
Dipping solution
Edible sugar pearls
Vegetable shortening
Cornstarch (cornflour) dusting bag
Peach 15mm (⅝in) ribbon
Circle cutters, 30mm (1¼in), 25mm (1in), 15mm (⅝in), 10mm (½in) and 8mm (¼in)
Large petal cutters in various sizes
Piping bag and piping nozzles (fine and extra-fine)
Ball tool
Set square
Foam mat
Kitchen paper
Stitching wheel
Parallel wheel cutter
Smooth-blade kitchen knife
Paintbrush
Royal icing
Non-toxic glue stick

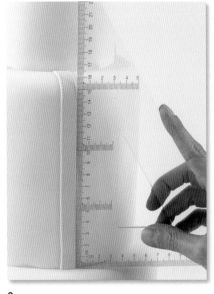

1. Using a parallel wheel cutter, cut two 8mm (¼in) strips of pale peach paste, each long enough to extend up the side of the 15cm (6in) deep tier and across the top to the base of the top tier. Run a stitch line along each side of each strip using the stitching wheel. Attach a strip to the front and back of the 15cm (6in) tier by first coating the cake underneath with water.

2. Use a set square to make sure the strip is straight, and adjust it if necessary by sliding it over the surface of the cake (not by removing it).

Tip

Ensure you use sufficient cake dowels to support each tier.

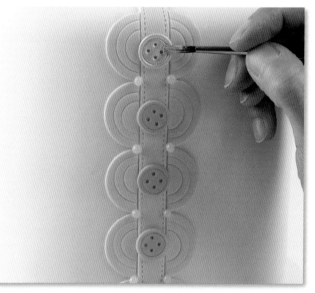

3. Cut numerous circles from pale peach paste using a 30mm (1¼in) circle cutter. Cut each one in half and emboss each semi-circle using two smaller cutters. Paint water onto the cake on either side of the two strips and attach the semi-circles as shown. Put the remaining semi-circles to one side.

4. Attach sugar pearls to the points where the shapes touch using dots of royal icing. Make twelve buttons using a 10mm (½in) circle cutter and emboss them with a slightly smaller cutter. Make the four tiny holes using the end of a fine piping nozzle. Attach the buttons to the cake as shown above. Keep two buttons back for finishing the statement flowers. Paint all the flowers with pearl lustre powder mixed with a little dipping solution.

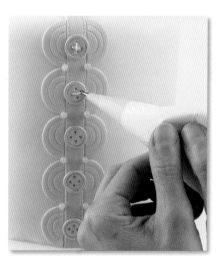

6. While they are still flexible, decorate the base of each tier with the remaining semi-circles, making more as required. Work from the bottom of the cake up, brushing the back of each shape with water before placing it on the cake. Use the paintbrush to manoeuvre the shapes into position. Finish with sugar pearls, as in step 4.

5. Use the extra-fine piping nozzle to add two thin threads of white royal icing across each button.

7. For each of the accent flowers, cut five petals from dark peach-coloured paste using the largest petal cutter. Working on a foam mat, create folds in the edges of the petals using the ball tool (see page 23).

8. Take a piece of kitchen paper, twist it into a tight sausage shape and curl it round to form a ring. Place your five petals evenly in the ring to form a flower shape. Stick the centres of the petals together using water and press down firmly in the centre of the flower to cup the petals before they dry.

9. Repeat steps 7 and 8 using a slightly smaller petal cutter and peach-coloured paste in a shade lighter. Secure these petals in the middle of the first set.

10. Repeat using a smaller petal cutter and the palest peach-coloured paste, and secure these in the flower centre. Finish with one of the buttons you made earlier.

11. Attach the two large flowers to the cake using large dots of royal icing applied to the backs.

BABY SHOWER

This cute pastel design is suitable for any newborn baby celebration. Basic cut-out shapes are transformed and embossed to form the pretty pram design and the coordinating base-board decoration. Begin by placing the cake in the centre of the board. Edge the cake with white ribbon secured with a small dot of royal icing on the join. Edge the board with yellow ribbon secured with non-toxic glue.

1. Cut out several 23mm (1in) circles from the pink, blue and green paste. Cut them in half and place them round the base of the cake.

2. To make the pram, first cut a circle from the blue paste using the largest cookie cutter. Cut it in half with a knife and trim away a segment from each side using the edge of the 35mm (1½in) cutter.

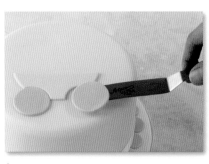

3. Position the pram centrally on the top of the cake. Cut two grey outer wheels using the 35mm (1½in) cookie cutter and place these on the cake. Use a palette knife to avoid over-handling the shapes.

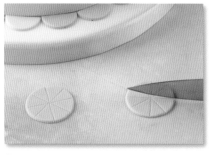

4. Cut two green circles using the 30mm (1¼in) cookie cutter and mark on the spokes using shallow cuts of the knife. Place these in the centre of the grey circles. Cut a green strip 86 x 5mm (3⅜ x ¼in) and position it along the top edge if the pram. For the hood, cut a pink circle using the 85mm (3⅜in) cutter and divide it into quarters. Mark radial spokes on one quarter using the knife and attach it to the cake.

Tip

To ensure the shapes stick securely, paint them with a light covering of water on the back just before positioning them on the cake.

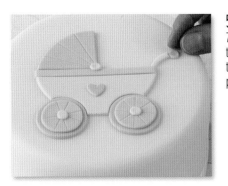

5. To finish, cut a little pink heart and three 7mm (¼in) yellow circles and position them on the cake. Use a curved off-cut for the handle, finished with a small circle of pink paste positioned on the end.

Tip

If you need to reposition a shape, don't try to remove it – simply slide it into its new position.

PANSY CAKE

This pansy design can be adapted for large and small cakes with ease. To get the right colours for the flowers, look at real pansies or find images on the internet and paint them in groups for a full and stunning effect. Once the cake has been decorated and put on the board, add double-sided tape round the cake and stick on the pale green ribbon, then more tape, then the spotted blue ribbon. Above the ribbon, add a decorative border punched out of sugar sheet with a craft border punch. Trim the board with just the spotted blue ribbon.

You will need

20.3cm (8in) cake and 3 cupcakes covered with sugarpaste (fondant)
25.4cm (10in) iced cake board
Edible powder food colours in bright blue, navy, white, lemon, yellow, dark green
Edible varnish
Brushes: 10mm (⅜in) flat, 6mm (¼in) flat, size 1 round
Pale green and spotted blue ribbon
Sugar sheet, craft border punch and edible glue

1. Pick up bright blue, navy and white on the 10mm (⅜in) brush and paint the top petals of the main pansies, and the buds.

2. Pick up lemon and navy and paint the green side petals.

3. Without cleaning the brush, pick up yellow and white and paint the lower petals.

4. Paint stems as on page 48 and scalloped leaves as on page 43, using dark green and white. Paint the bracts around the buds using flat leaf brush strokes (see page 42).

5. Use the 6mm (¼in) flat brush to add small green and yellow-green flat leaves to the design.

The finished Pansy Cake with cupcakes. These show how you can paint part of the main design – one pansy, two pansies or two buds – to create beautiful cupcakes for any occasion, or to complement your main cake for a big celebration (see detail above).

6. Paint dots in the centres of the pansies with the end of the brush handle and yellow and white, using the technique shown on page 46.

7. Pick up navy and white on the 6mm (¼in) flat brush and touch the pansies close to the centres to create stamens.

Below and opposite
Details from the cake and cupcakes.

8. Dilute dark green with lots of varnish and use a size 1 round brush to paint tendrils, as shown on page 48.

SUMMER BUNTING

This cake is perfect for a summer tea party or a vintage-style fair. It is accompanied by matching cupcakes and displayed on an easy-to-make cake stand. The design uses modelling paste to capture the look of bunting blowing in the breeze, and edible transfers for an easy and eye-catching effect.

To display the cake, use two boards covered with white sugarpaste (fondant), and emboss the larger board with a pattern of small circles round the edge, marked on using an 11mm (½in) circle cutter. Both boards are edged with white ribbon, secured with non-toxic glue, then a narrower turquoise ribbon has been placed over the white ribbon on the smaller board. Begin by positioning the cake in the centre of the smaller board and edging the base with white ribbon secured with a dot of royal icing on the join.

1. Cut numerous small white circles from white modelling paste using the 11mm (½in) circle cutter. Attach them to the rim of the cake using water. To attach them in an even circle, place a round cake tin on top of the cake and work round it.

2. Cut an 8cm (3¼in) deep strip of baking parchment, long enough to fit once round the cake. Fold it into eight sections, draw a curve on the top edge and cut along the curve.

You will need

You will need
15cm (6in) round fruit or sponge cake covered with white sugarpaste (fondant)
20.5cm (8in) round drum board covered with white sugarpaste (fondant)
10cm (4in) round polystyrene cake divider
30.5cm (12in) drum board covered with white sugarpaste (fondant) for base
9 cupcakes covered with white sugarpaste (fondant), baked in pink cupcake cases
Small amounts of pink, light brown, white and red modelling paste
Edible transfers in pink, turquoise and green polka dot design
Vegetable shortening
Cornstarch (cornflour) dusting bag
Turquoise 10mm (½in) ribbon
White 15mm (⅝in) ribbon
13cm (5in) round cake tin
Circle cutters, 15mm (⅝in), 11mm (½in) and 7mm (¼in)
Square cutters, 16mm (⅝in) and 11mm (½in)
Rectangular cutter, 25 x 14mm (1 x ⅝in)
Square cookie cutters, 50mm (2in), 45mm (1¾in) and 40mm (1½in)
Round cookie cutter, 35mm (1½in)
Smooth-blade kitchen knife
Scribing tool
Fine piping nozzle
Baking parchment
Masking tape
Scissors
Paintbrush
Royal icing
Small cranked palette knife
Non-toxic glue stick
Metal ruler
Paper tissue

3. Unfold the template round the cake with the straight edge at the base and secure the ends with a strip of masking tape. Steady the template with your hand and mark a thin line along the curved edge with the scribing tool.

4. Fix transfer sheets to rolled-out modelling paste and cut out numerous flags using the rectangular cutter. Use the corner of the cutter to cut a triangle out of one side of each rectangle to make a flag shape. Also cut out four circles using the 11mm (½in) circle cutter and four using the 15mm (⅝in) circle cutter. Cut each one in half with the knife to create the little cupcake decorations on top of the cake. Put these to one side.

5. While they are still flexible, attach the flags to the side of the cake following the scribed line. To secure each flag, brush a strip of water along the short, straight edge, then place a tiny piece of paper tissue under the flag to hold it away from the cake while it is drying. This will create an impression of movement. Place one of the little triangles that you cut from the flags in step 4 at the top of each swag.

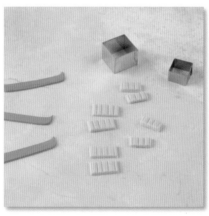

6. Use each of the three square cookie cutters to cut three squares of pink modelling paste. Using one side of the cutter, cut strips with slightly curved edges.

7. Use the 16mm (⅝in) and 11mm (½in) square cutters to cut four squares (two of each size) of light brown modelling paste, then cut each one in half using a knife to make the cake bases. Mark on the lines with the knife.

8. For the cherries, roll eight tiny balls of red paste. Make the handle for the cake stand by cutting a tiny circle using the 7mm (¼in) circle cutter, and removing a pink circle from the centre using a piping nozzle. Finally, cut two thin lengths of pink modelling paste and trim them to lengths 2.5cm (1in) for the base of the cake stand and 2cm (¾in) for the handle.

9. Arrange all the elements of the cake stand on the top of the cake, using the palette knife to position them accurately. Make sure the cake stand is positioned in the centre of the cake. Paint the back of each shape with water before placing it on the cake, and reposition elements by sliding them rather than taking them off and replacing them.

10. Decorate the cupcakes using circles cut from the edible transfer sheets using the 35mm (1½in) round cookie cutter, and hand-rolled balls of red modelling paste.

11. To display the cake, place it on the cake divider placed in the centre of the larger drum board, and place the cupcakes round it.

SUMMER ROSES

Roses are the essence of summer and this design makes a perfect party or anniversary cake. Additional cupcakes allow you to indulge yourself in painting when painting one cake simply isn't enough, and they add to the impact of the display. Once the cake has been decorated and put on the board, add double-sided tape around the cake, stick the first, widest ribbon to this, then repeat this process on top of this ribbon, and then again with the narrowest ribbon. Complete by adding the ribbon bows. Trim the board with narrow purple ribbon too.

You will need
25.4cm (10in) cake and 3 cupcakes, all covered with sugarpaste (fondant)
30.5cm (12in) iced cake board
Edible powder food colours in cherry red, burgundy, white, dark green and citrus green
Edible varnish
Brushes: 10mm (⅜in) flat
Wide purple ribbon, narrower deep pink ribbon and narrower still pale green ribbon for the cake
Narrow purple ribbon for the board

1. Paint the outer petals of the roses as shown on pages 46–47 with mixes of cherry red and white, and burgundy and white. Continue round the cake. Leave two of the roses half completed as shown, as one rose is partly behind another, and one will be partly covered with leaves.

Opposite
The finished cake with cupcakes. One has three roses in autumn shades, using pinks and oranges, with some brown leaves. Another has rosebuds (see page 47) in the same shades as the cake, and the third has a dense pattern of roses in summer shades.

2. Paint the centres of the roses as shown on pages 46–47.

3. Continue adding petals to the roses as shown on pages 46–47.

4. Paint large, dark green scalloped leaves as shown on page 43, then add more in citrus green. Some of the leaves should just go over the edge of the cake as shown.

6. Add smaller flat leaves as shown.

5. Continue adding large scalloped leaves.

Opposite
Detail of the cupcakes.

DAISY CAKE

You can vary the colours of the daisies to suit your colour scheme with this beautiful flower-shaped cake. Decorating the iced cake board by painting with daisies is a lovely finishing touch. Simply use a smaller brush to paint smaller flowers. The daisy designs look great on cupcakes too. Trim the cake with a border punched from sugar sheet using a craft border punch. To ice the board, roll out sugarpaste (fondant), dampen the board slightly so the sugarpaste (fondant) will stick, then roll the sugarpaste (fondant) on to the board and cut to size. Once you have completed the cake, run double-sided tape round the board and stick the ribbon to this.

You will need
25.4cm (10in) flower-shaped cake and 3 cupcakes, all covered with sugarpaste (fondant)
30.5cm (12in) iced cake board
Edible powder food colours in primrose yellow, white, orange, brown, citrus green
Edible varnish
Brushes: 6mm (¼in) flat, size 5 round, size 1 round
Yellow ribbon
Sugar sheet, craft border punch and edible glue

1. The daisy design is demonstrated here on a cupcake, but the same one is used on the main cake. Use the 6mm (¼in) brush to paint petals in primrose yellow and white, then paint petals in orange and white over and in between them.

2. Use a size 5 round brush cut for stippling (see page 45) to stipple the centre with brown.

3. Use the 6mm (¼in) flat brush to paint the lines on the petals, using the chisel edge of the brush dipped in orange.

4. Use the size 1 round brush to paint white dots of highlight in the centre. Add flat leaves (see page 42) in citrus green and white.

Right: detail from the finished cakes. The top of the main cake has been decorated with daisies and half-daisies. The iced board is also covered with daisies. The cupcakes have a variety of daisy designs.

SINGLE TIER CAKE WITH DAISY FLOWERS

This cake has been decorated using a spot lustre technique which can be adapted to large and small cakes with ease. Contrasting colours work well together to create a dramatic effect.

You will need

Floral Burst stencil

30cm (12in) round cake covered with white sugarpaste (fondant)

10mm (⅜in), 12mm (½in), and 15mm (⅝in) flat brushes

Edible dusting powder in white, yellow, light green, dark green, purple and pearl white

Kitchen paper

Large rolling pin

White vegetable fat

1. Place your stencil on top of the iced cake and emboss the design into the surface using a rolling pin.

2. Begin to establish the base image by colouring the tips of the leaves near the narrow-petalled flower with light green edible dusting powder and the 12mm (½in) flat brush.

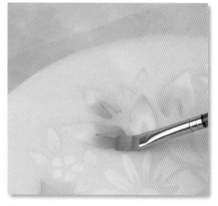

3. Without cleaning the brush, build up the stems and bases of some of the leaves to create some shading using the dark green powder.

4. Change to a clean 15mm (⅝in) brush and use purple powder to colour the flowers. Put the brush to one side.

5. Change to a 10mm (⅜in) flat brush. Pick up yellow on the brush and colour the petals of the third foreground flower, working from the outside in. Pick up a little white on the brush when you reload to soften the colour a little.

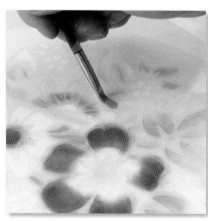

The finished Single Tier Cake with Daisy Flowers, along with two cupcakes decorated using the same techniques and a smaller complementary stencil.

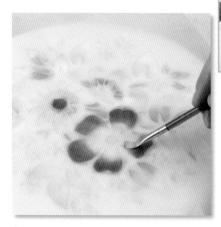

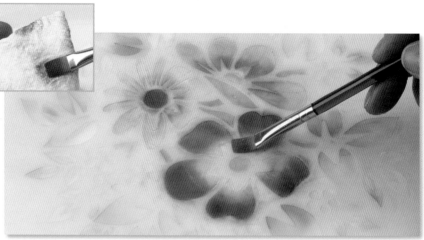

6. Pick up an even mix of white and yellow on the same brush and colour the smaller background flowers. Without cleaning the brush, pick up white and colour the remaining parts of the foreground flowers.

7. Pick up the brush with a little purple remaining on it (from step 4), and gently blend the colours together on the foreground flowers. The tiny amount of colour remaining on the brush will softly tint the petals. As the colour runs out, you will need to reload the brush with purple. Wipe away most of the powder on kitchen paper to ensure you retain a subtle effect (see inset).

8. Still using the same brush, use a sweeping motion to begin to blend the leaves together. Sweep the brush across the tips of a whole group of leaves to bind them together and give a cohesive feel. Differentiating the leaves across the design helps add depth to the design.

9. Pick up a little purple and light green on the brush and mix them together on a spare lid or the work surface. Use a little of this mix to soften any particularly strong colours remaining on the design, such as the very bright yellow background flowers.

10. With the blending completed, very gently overlay the whole image with pearl white and a light circular motion to soften the colour a little more, then carefully remove the stencil to finish (see inset).

Opposite
Details from the Daisy Flower cake and cupcakes decorated in a similar way.

FALLING LEAVES

This seasonally inspired design uses freehand wheel cutting and texturing techniques to create a beautiful autumn tree. A leaf cutter and veiner add texture to the leaves. To start, edge the board with brown ribbon and secure it with non-toxic glue. Position the cake in the centre of the board.

You will need

15cm (6in) round fruit or sponge cake covered with white sugarpaste (fondant)
20.5cm (8in) round drum board covered with green sugarpaste (fondant)
Small amounts of brown modelling paste
Small amounts or red, orange, yellow, beige and rust-coloured gum paste (flower paste)
Vegetable shortening
Cornstarch (cornflour) dusting bag
Brown 15mm (⅝in) ribbon
Round cookie cutters, 85mm (3⅜in) and 65mm (2½in)
Rose leaf cutter, 11mm (½in)
Rose leaf silicone veiner
Wheel cutter
Smooth-blade kitchen knife
Paintbrush
Royal icing
Piping bag and fine piping nozzle
Small cranked palette knife
Non-toxic glue stick

1. Make a long, thin sausage shape using the brown modelling paste and attach it round the base of the cake. Emboss it using the wheel cutter to resemble tree bark.

2. Cut two large brown circles using the 85mm (3⅜in) and 65mm (2½in) cookie cutters. Trim off the sides of the smaller circle using the same cutter to form the trunk.

3. Use the 85mm (3⅜in) cookie cutter to create a curve at the top of the trunk for the tree top to sit in. With the wheel cutter, cut out sections from the tree top to resemble branches.

4. Fuse the trunk to the top of the tree by rubbing both edges with water using your finger and pushing them together.

5. Cut into the branches using the wheel cutter to create finer branches, and cut a wavy line across the base of the trunk, again using the wheel cutter. Soften the join between the tree trunk and top using a paintbrush.

6. Brush off any loose sugar and add texture to the tree by marking it using the wheel cutter.

7. Using the rose leaf cutter, cut numerous leaves from orange, yellow, beige and rust-coloured gum paste (flower paste). Mark on the veins using the rose leaf silicone veiner. Roll several red berries by hand.

8. Fix the tree to the top of the cake with a little water brushed on the back. Then arrange the leaves on the cake and fix by piping tiny dots of royal icing behind each of them. Finally, fix some of the leaves and berries round the base and down the side of the cake. Place the leaves at various angles, overlapping them and attaching them at the base only so they stand proud of the cake. This creates a three-dimensional effect.

Make coordinating cupcakes to go with your cake if you wish – simply decorated with leaves and berries.

LAVENDER CUPCAKES

If you have never tried painting on cakes before, these quick and easy cupcakes would be a good place to start. Simple stems of lavender crisscrossing over each other to form tiny bunches are the essence of the design. You could even use real lavender to flavour the cupcakes. Tint the sugarpaste (fondant) with edible powder food colours, using the mix described in step 2, and varying the strength between cupcakes.

You will need

Five cupcakes covered with sugarpaste (fondant) tinted with lilac edible powder food colours in various strengths
Edible powder food colours in citrus green, white, navy blue, cherry red, lilac blue
Edible varnish
Brushes: 6mm (¼in) flat

1. Use the 6mm (¼in) flat brush with citrus green and white to paint stems on the sugarpaste (fondant) plaque on top of the cupcake.

2. To make an edible lilac paint, mix navy blue, cherry red and lilac blue with white. Mix this to a shade darker than your sugarpaste (fondant) plaque and use the tip of the brush to print little lavender flower shapes.

3. Build up the pattern of the lavender, working your way down the outside edges of the stems.

Opposite
The finished cupcakes. These beautiful cupcakes would make a beautiful spread at a summer wedding or party. Vary the tones of the purples and greens.

4. Reload the brush and paint more lavender flowers down the middles of the stems.

5. Paint more little flowers at the bottom over the stems.

6. Go back and paint more citrus green and white foliage below the flowers.

Details of the Lavender Cupcakes.

PATTERNED CUPCAKES

This simple technique – of interchanging different coloured icing in a pattern on a small cupcake – creates a stunning and unusual effect. Experiment with your colours to get a different look every time.

You will need

Vintage Flock stencil
1 or more cupcakes
Edible dusting powder in metallic blue
Green and blue sugarpaste (fondant)
Smoother
Rolling pin and spacers
15mm (⅝in) flat brush
Circle cutter and kitchen knife
White vegetable fat

1. Cover the surface with white vegetable fat and roll out green sugarpaste (fondant), using spacers to ensure the depth is uniform. Trim away the side with a sharp kitchen knife to leave a straight edge.

2. Roll out and trim your blue sugarpaste (fondant) in the same way and abut the pieces. Use a smoother to gently bond them together into a uniform surface.

3. Place the stencil on top of the sugarpaste (fondant) surface and firmly roll over it.

4. Use a 15mm (⅝in) flat brush with metallic blue edible dusting powder to colour an area of the stencil large enough to cut out, then remove the stencil.

5. Use the circle cutter to cut out a circle, then place it on top of the cupcake.

Detail from the Patterned Cupcakes, shown opposite. This technique is easily adapted to give a striped effect, by trimming one colour into a thin strip and abutting pieces on either side, or to give a patchwork effect by smoothing small squares together.

Opposite

The finished cupcake alongside others made with the same techniques. Vintage Flock, Filigree Swirl, Vibrant Vines, Rose and Swirly stencils were used with various colours and combinations of sugarpaste (fondant) pieces.

LACY CUPCAKES

These cupcakes are created using a simple blending technique. When blending, always ensure you use the lightest colour first. Clean your brush between each application to keep the colours sharp and stop them muddying.

You will need

Butterfly Lace stencil
1 or more cupcakes
White sugarpaste (fondant)
Edible dusting powder in metallic red and gold
5mm (¼in) flat brush
7.5cm (3in) circle cutter
Spacers and rolling pin
White vegetable fat

 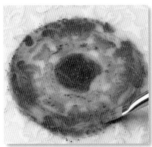  

1. Cover the surface with white vegetable fat and roll out white sugarpaste (fondant), using spacers to ensure the depth is uniform. Use the roller to emboss the surface with the stencil, ensuring the focal point of the design is central on your icing.

2. Use the 5mm (¼in) flat brush to colour the centre (or focal point) with dusting powder. Start in the centre with metallic red, then circle this with gold without cleaning your brush. Repeat for the outer part with metallic red.

3. Carefully remove the stencil and place the circle cutter on top, ensuring the focal point is in the exact centre.

4. Use the circle cutter to cut out the icing and place it on top of the cupcake.

Right

Detail from the Lacy Cupcakes, shown opposite. By altering where you put the colours, a variety of blended designer cupcakes can be made.

TEMPLATES

PIPING BASIC SHAPES

All templates are shown full size except
where stated otherwise.

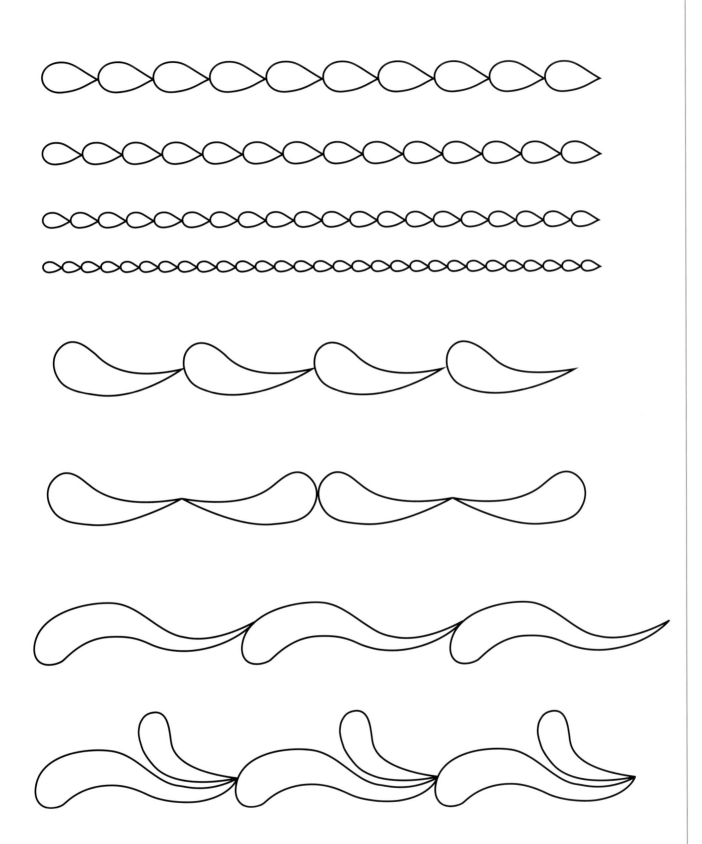

TOY TRAIN, PAGES 54–57

Half actual size – copy at 200%

Sky

Ground

MODERN BLACKWORK, PAGES 72–79

Template A

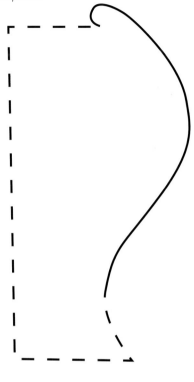

MODERN BLACKWORK, PAGES 72–79

Butterfly and primrose templates

MODERN BLACKWORK, PAGES 72–79

Leaf templates

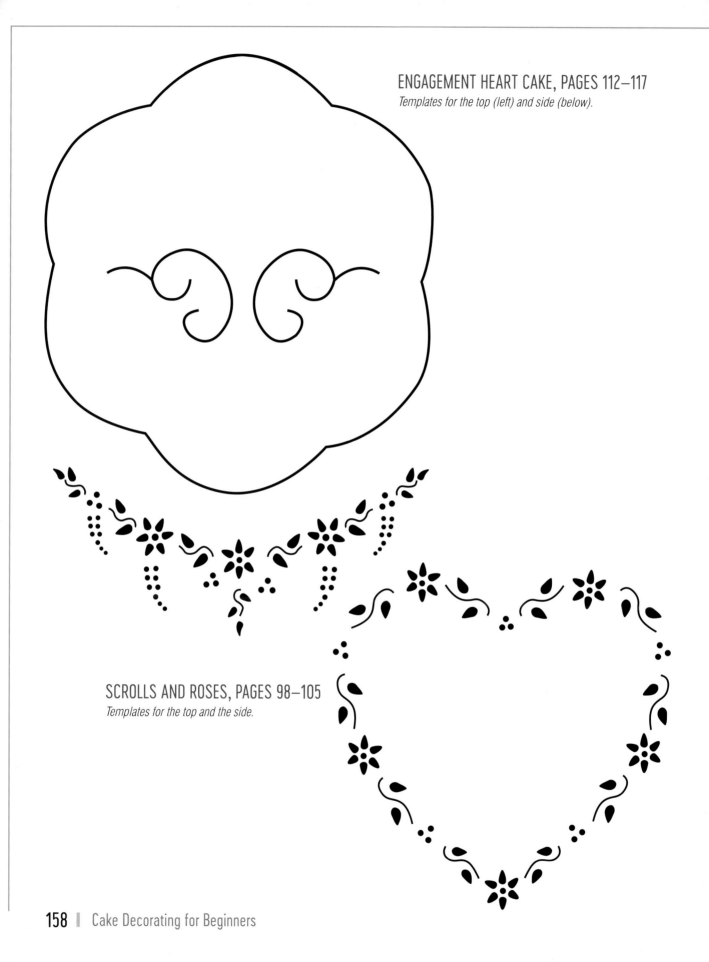

ENGAGEMENT HEART CAKE, PAGES 112–117
Templates for the top (left) and side (below).

SCROLLS AND ROSES, PAGES 98–105
Templates for the top and the side.

INDEX

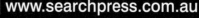